Birth Control and Catholics

Birth Control and Catholics

Msgr. GEORGE A. KELLY

Doubleday & Company, Inc.
Garden City, New York, 1963

Nihil obstat: John A. Goodwine, J.C.D.
                  Censor Librorum

Imprimatur: ✠Francis Cardinal Spellman
                 Archbishop of New York
                 July 5, 1963

The *nihil obstat* and *imprimatur* are official declarations that a book or pamphlet is free of doctrinal or moral error. No implication is contained therein that those who have granted the *nihil obstat* and *imprimatur* agree with the contents, opinions, or statements expressed.

DEDICATED TO
His Excellency
The Most Rev. John J. Maguire, D.D., V.G.
Auxiliary Bishop of New York

Contents

Introduction

THERE are few subjects which stir up more controversy in the United States than birth control. Even teen-agers, far removed from the real problems of life, have strong feelings on the subject. To some, the word "contraception" represents salvation of one kind or another; to others, it has become a symbol of all that is wrong with modern marriage.

Much of the blame for the tension over birth control is laid at the door of the Catholic Church. They say: If only priests and bishops, particularly that one in Rome, would stop making a fuss about it, the majority of Americans could use their contraceptives with a far easier conscience.

Certainly, Catholic opinion on this matter is, *at the present time,* minority opinion. It was not always so and may not be so in the foreseeable future. Part of the heat engendered by the ever continuing American dialogue on birth control means that the evangelists of contraception have not won their day as completely as they would like. After all, despite the availability of all kinds of pills, jellies, and devices, we do have one of the highest birth rates in the Western World. The Planned Parenthood

Federation of America may believe that Catholics and
non-Catholics agree on the desirability of family limitation but really argue only over methods. This, in my
judgment, is an oversimplified view of the situation.

Involved in any birth control controversy is a whole
philosophy of sex, marriage, and parenthood. Christian
marriage is not defined exclusively by the production or
elimination of babies. When sexual satisfaction is completely divorced from the basic reason for sexual faculties
in the first place, then the marriage relationship has an
entirely different significance than when the couple always relate sex to parenthood, even when they are not
contemplating pregnancy.

Admittedly, the Catholic husband and wife working
out their marriage in a culture somewhat hostile to Christian family values will face critical decisions, if not early
in their life together, then sometime after their tenth anniversary. Should we have a child right away? How many
should we have? What about spacing? Is there ever really
such a person as the unwanted child? Suppose husband
and wife disagree? If births are regulated, how can one
do this and still uphold moral values? Is not continence
for the married unthinkable?

These are some of the questions we hope to discuss for
Catholic married couples in this book. But the book may
be discovered by non-Catholics. They like babies just as
much as we do. Many of them face the same problem of
raising a large family. They are concerned about contraception, too. What started out as help in an emergency
has become a rule of life for a whole society. Even the
young have picked it up. They see that the approval
originally given conditionally to a device is now being ex-

tended to sterilization and abortion. And so they wonder and take a second look at our rates of promiscuity, illegitimacy, adultery, and divorce.

Many minds and hands went into the planning and production of this book, not the least of which belong to Msgr. John C. Knott, national Family Life Director, Dr. Edward Keefe of St. Vincent's Hospital, New York City and Dr. Claude Lanctot, formerly of the Chicago Lying-In Hospital, John and Margaret McPartland, Gerald and Eileen Fitzgerald, Woodrow and Helen Wolff of New York's Christian Family Movement. Most of all, my special gratitude and affection to Mr. John Springer, member of the Advisory Board of the Family Life Bureau, who worked closely, intelligently, and devotedly with the author during a year of research and writing.

GEORGE A. KELLY

1.

What Marriage Is all About

WHEN a Catholic man and woman stand at the altar of God to seal their sacred contract of matrimony, together they pledge themselves to one of the noblest vocations it is possible for human beings to undertake. Holding each other's hand, they set up in God's presence and with God's help a little community all their own. Like pioneers and conquerors, whose legendary feats make the pages of history interesting, they carve out a small part of God's Kingdom, put their name on it, and agree evermore to expend all their energies to make it grow and prosper. And because they themselves already have on their souls the MARK of CHRIST in Baptism, this particular marital union is far more important than just another family. Their home is to be a "Little Church." They are to be its bishops. Their work is to be supernatural as well as natural, redemptive as well as creative. And their destiny is happiness hereafter as well as in this life.

This conjugal union, however, is not of their own exclusive making. It arises out of the pact that man and woman make with God. He commands them to love each other, to share a common home and a common bed, to foreswear all other entanglements, to be faithful, and to live together "for better and for worse until death do them part." He empowers them to engage in sexual activity and He gives them primary rights over the children that might issue from their marriage.

Because life together looks so attractive, marriage is desirable and possible. God first made man male and female, endowing each sex with special characteristics, each sex reflecting God in a special way, and then he joins them "two in one flesh" as if the married couple best reflects all that is good in humanity. People come to marriage with this expectation. They find in the common life the comfort, consolation, and companionship that foreshadows their eternal union with God in heaven. The bliss of the honeymoon is such a beautiful thing because it represents so much giving, so much innocence, so much hope. Loneliness and pain disappear with the first ecstasy. And the possibility that one day they will mold and fashion a human soul to their own image and likeness, as much as to God's, gives them a sense of importance unrealized by many of the world's most powerful men.

All this is theirs because God wants them to have it. Naturally, growth does not come smoothly. A vocation involving the uniting in mind, heart, and affection of two basically different sexes is far more difficult for some to achieve successfully than others. But if failures come, it will be their fault—not God's. And even if their union never meets Divine expectations, it still stands because marriage and family life are too important to man and God to permit it to be battered to and fro by the winds of human fickleness or passion. The original pact with God stands as long as both of them shall live.

Weak men and wicked men have made many efforts to destroy marriage throughout history. Before and after Christ, pagans of all kinds have made assaults on marriage and on those who defend God's stake in marriage. Whether the attack was made on the permanency of any union between one man and one woman, or on childbearing or on fidelity or involved the glorification of sexual passion for its own sake, or accentuated unduly the dominance of male over female or female over male, the end result has always been the same—the denial of God's rights, and intense suffering for husbands and wives as well as children.

Naturally, some of the objections to Christian marriage are given a plausible guise. Heart-rending examples of terrible hardship imposed by strict morality are given ample telling. And we must admit that such sad situations exist now and will exist until the end of time. Life is unequal and some bear greater crosses than others. This is the mysterious problem of evil to which men in this life will never find an adequate answer. But most human crises are of man's own making. Relieving them at the expense of God's guidelines by which all of us should live, has proven more costly in the end. A cursory glance around us clearly documents the truth that good people do well even, if not especially, under trying circumstances.

Therefore let us appreciate the beauty and importance of a man's union with his wife, because God would not have it otherwise. Let married couples strive with every fiber of their being to fulfill all the anticipation of their honeymoon. Let their happiness pervade mind, heart, will, soul, and body of one as much as the other, and more importantly of both together. Let them grow old gracefully, content on their golden jubilee that they belong together. Let death leave an empty void in the spouse left behind, one which only death a second time can fill.

But—and here we touch a great argument between Christ and the Church on one side and the world on the other—let them realize that the union of marriage is not an end in itself, that they were made "two in one flesh" for a purpose far beyond anything they could conceive as human beings.

For the conjugal union of marriage was established by God that through it, indeed because of it, He would be glorified with new children, whose creation and redemption become, not only His work, but theirs.

Unless we realize that the basic purpose of marital union is parenthood, we do not know what marriage is all about. Husband and wife, regardless of why they came, leave the altar of their wedding with a mission—to give life, to fashion life, to sanctify life, so that on the last day they can return to God the fruits of their handiwork.

We stress this point because outside of the Catholic world, a new definition of marriage is being offered, even by ministers of the gospel, a new viewpoint that finds no justification in reason, revelation, or the history of Judaism or Christianity. New prophets say: "The couple comes first. Pope Pius XI is wrong when he says 'Among the blessings of marriage, the child holds first place.' If chil-

dren interfere with personal fulfillment or become oner-
ous, they are to be excluded."

Let us take a look at this child who creates so many
problems.

THE SON OF HIS PARENTS

Marriage is both a responsibility and a privilege. It both
requires and enables a man and woman to participate in
the act of conception—a work which humbles even the
proudest of men. Who of us, of his own power, could
create anything so magnificent as a tiny baby? It is recorded that the great Michelangelo was almost reduced
to tears when he looked upon his thrillingly lifelike statue
of Moses upon its completion in Florence around 1513.
Overawed he was by his own creation, but at his moment
of greatest ecstasy he realized that his accomplishment
could not be compared with what could be accomplished
by a simple peasant woman giving birth to a living soul.

This act of conception is one which even the world's
finest scientific minds cannot fully comprehend. It is
truly an awesome thing for a husband and wife to realize
that from an act which expresses their mutual love will
grow a human being also capable of love, thought, and
prayer—that from their bond of love can emerge a soul
destined to live for all eternity.

Bringing babies into the world, and caring for them
so that they may be good and responsible men and women
when they grow up, is the first work of marriage. It
was to provide the means of which children could be
born and educated to populate His Kingdom, that God

created this institution. This is a necessary work—one which must be done if the human race is to survive, and if human beings are to be brought into this world so that they might gain an eternal place with the Creator in heaven.

This is what parenthood means—that the hand of God has reached down from the heavens to touch the marriage bed in a special way, to give the wife's cells joined with her husband's an individually created soul whereby their child can love, think, and pray and go back to God from whence he came. Parents are indeed blessed, because God chooses them to become His intimate collaborators in creating a new being whose life story will never end.

God does not need you to bring human beings to the world. He could select an endless number of possibilities by which a child could be created. But if He does designate you to create a child He wants to have born, this collaboration will be your benediction.

A parent's collaboration with God does not end with the birth. Then begins the task of molding the human being—a task which is of the greatest importance if God's purpose in allowing the child to be conceived is to be realized.

We know that the bearing and educating of children is the work of marriage from the natures of man and woman and from the needs of the newborn baby himself. For only through the God-implanted organs of man and woman, acting together, can life be conceived. And it is through the family, with the father as its head and the mother as its heart, that the infant can best receive the particular love, understanding, and guidance he needs to learn what he must do to reach a responsible adulthood and ultimately to save his soul.

We know also that parenthood is the work of marriage because God told us so. He spoke to all mankind when He blessed Adam and Eve with these words: "Increase and multiply, and fill the earth." (Genesis, 1:28.)

And it was clear that Adam knew why God gave him Eve as his helpmate and companion. For it became Adam's duty to bestow a name upon her. He might have chosen names signifying friend, companion, sweetheart, or any other term of endearment. Instead, he called her Eve—a word meaning mother. "And Adam called the name of his wife, Eve, because she was the Mother of all the living." (Genesis, 3:20.)

PARENTS ARE BLESSED BY GOD

This idea of man and woman united in the common work of parenthood has endured through history in the way it is viewed by Catholics today. As a responsibility, to be sure, but also as one of the greatest of privileges that man can have.

So great a privilege was it considered in Old Testament days, for example, that having children was regarded as a sign of God's favor. The man with many children was considered among the richest of men and the most blessed in His sight. The Israelites deemed as one of the greatest of gifts, that which God gave to Abraham when He said: "I will make thy seed as the dust of the earth." (Genesis, 13:16.) It is also recorded in the Bible that the Lord promised that if the Jews obeyed His "precepts and ceremonies and judgments" that "no one shall be barren among you." (Deuteronomy, 7:11, 14.) The Book of Proverbs reads: "Crown of old age, when a man sees his children's children; pride of youth, when a man can boast of the fathers that begot him." (17, 6.) In fact, among the Jews the inability to have children was a mark of God's disfavor.

Parenthood as a means of helping husbands and wives to save their souls also was recognized in New Testament times. For example, St. Paul advised women to "marry, bear children," lest "being idle they learn to go about from house to house, and are not only idle but tattlers also, and busybodies, mentioning things which they ought not." (1 Timothy, 5:13–14.) Moreover, St. Paul said, woman "shall be saved through childbearing; if she continue in faith, and love, and sanctification, with sobriety," (1 Timothy, 2:15.) Down through the years, the Church has taught that in educating their children the parents themselves would indeed draw closer to God. In fact, the spiritual, emotional and physical advantages of parenthood can hardly be overestimated.

Parenthood means spiritual growth because God infuses their child with a soul that will live forever. Thus from the very beginning their work becomes a work for eternity. Long after the things of the world are ashes, after man's greatest works have turned to dust, the human soul they bring to life will live on and on.

In doing this work with God, parents gain a vision of the purpose and meaning of existence. As they consider their responsibilities towards their child, they realize how vain and useless are the things of this life unless they are used as a means of attaining lasting union with God in heaven.

In teaching their child to know God and to do His will, parents themselves learn about Him anew. Seeing God through a child's eyes, they also see Him in a new light. And just as their child has faith that they will care for him with love, so too do they realize that they must place their own complete trust in God the Father. They gain a new insight into what Jesus meant when He said, "Let the little children be, and do not hinder them from coming to Me, for of such is the Kingdom of Heaven." (Matthew, 19:14.) We all must become as little children in the eyes of God, completely accepting His will, if we are to gain salvation.

As parents strive to protect their own child with tenderness and mercy, they realize too how their Heavenly Father protects and provides for them. It has often been said that a man does not appreciate the sacrifices his parents made for him until he becomes a parent himself. It is also true that when he serves as protector of his own child, he gains a stronger sense of his relationship with Our Eternal Father upon Whom we all utterly depend.

Parenthood also strengthens the emotional development of husbands and wives. How often do we observe formerly self-centered young men and young women, interested only in their own pleasures, as they become serious, sacrificing fathers and mothers. Possibly for the first time they realize that it is more blessed to give than to receive. Also possibly for the first time, they understand the meaning of sacrifice—the true joy that results from quelling one's own desires for the welfare of others.

Now they began to understand the full meaning of love. For their love for their child strengthens their love for each other. 'Thus a child is both the fruit of love and its source, and in working together for their children's welfare, the man and wife are united in a bond that grows stronger every day. Their joys and sacrifices, triumphs and disappointments as the child moves from the crib into childhood, adolescence, and adulthood— these all contribute not only to their love for the child, but also to their own love. In recognizing the importance of tenderness to a child, they learn how important it is for each other.

True, there are exceptions. Some men and women fail to develop love for each other in marriage. But when this happens, it will generally be found that at least one of the partners insists upon retaining his or her self-centeredness, and will not make the sacrifices that a harmonious marriage always requires. Such people actually resist the spirit of married love. They cannot fully love another because they are too deeply in love with themselves.

On the practical level (the level so appealing to moderns) the satisfactions of parenthood are regarded as one of the great experiences of life. They give it meaning: they offer parents a goal to work for together, a vision to hold before themselves as they strive to make their children educated, responsible citizens.

But what more than anything else makes parenthood a joy is perhaps the realization that fathers and mothers are engaging in the molding of the mind and heart of another human being. For the mother and father are the child's foremost teachers. What he will be in life will depend, more than anything else, upon the influences of his own home. What your child thinks and how he acts about God, the Church, his fellowman, will reflect your own teaching and example more than anything else to which he will be exposed. It is this opportunity to take living clay and mold it as you choose that literally makes the education of a child a more engrossing, more demanding, and more interesting work than any in which even the greatest of creative artists—men like Michelangelo—are able to achieve. It is a great truism that a man's epitaph is written in the lives of the children he has left behind.

As your children grow and respond to your care, you will see the results of your teaching. In living with them, you will recover your own childhood. You will begin to look at the world with a new sense of wide-eyed wonder as they do, seeing mystery and beauty in the ordinary things of life which for other adults have paled into insignificance.

CHILDREN MAKE THE HOME

It is your children who will make your home. They will transform it into a little tabernacle, where you and they join together with an ideal of family life modeled after the Holy Family of Nazareth.

The Holy Family, like all human families, had its sad moments and its happy ones. But after the Incarnation, Mary and Joseph knew that their work was to serve God's will and therefore they devoted themselves completely to the work He assigned to them. They knew

their destiny as you should know yours, and this knowledge gave them the strength to make every sacrifice required of them. Their life, devoted to the Child Jesus,
was in opposition to the teaching of the modern world
that children exist to "fulfill" the parents. Mary and
Joseph lived for their Child.

In a home built upon this model, there will be found
higher moral standards—for who would not be a better
person when he realized that he is giving an example
to an innocent child? Home is where your children will
come to know God, where they will observe His influence
in the daily life of prayer, good works, and Christian love
for one another. A home with children, therefore, will be
where both you and your offspring have the best possible
environment in which to work out your destiny and save
your immortal souls.

The Catholic family symbolizes the mystical body of
Christ. The father, as its head, represents Our Lord.
The wife represents the Church, and the children, as
members of the body, the faithful. Through the common
life of the family, all the members worship God and
express their submission to Him.

The family also helps Christ to redeem its members
in the world. For when Our Lord made marriage a
Sacrament, he established the family as the channel
through which to give His grace to men. The husband and wife channel grace to each other and to their
children, and vice versa.

THE FAMILY WITH MANY CHILDREN

The advantages children bring to the home can often be seen most distinctly in the family with many children. In such a home there is indeed a small community—a society in microcosm—in which the virtues of selflessness, consideration, and concern for the welfare of others must be practiced. It is here that the parents develop a great sense of self-sacrifice for the welfare of their children, and where the children learn to sacrifice their own interests so that their brothers and sisters may benefit as well.

Rare indeed is the selfish child who has known life in a large family. Unlike the only child in a family who can make himself the center of attention and can manipulate his parents into doing what he wishes, the child in a large family is but one of many, and he must learn that others have rights equal to his own. Let him insist upon his own way and the pursuit of his own selfish ends, and his own brothers and sisters will devise suitable ways of teaching him the error of his ways.

Another advantage of many children is that they teach each other the importance of observing rules set down for the common good. There is evidence to be seen all around them of the importance that attaches to the methods of doing things which have been set down for the family at large.

The greatest practical value of the large family is its educational advantages to both parents and children. As their children grow, parents delight in watching their various and interesting stages of development which mark

new milestones on the child's road to maturity. And when
the youngest child is no longer a baby but trudges off to
school, the oldest children may become fathers and
mothers themselves, giving their own parents an opportunity to participate once more in observing the marvelous
story of human growth and development.

Regardless of how old their children are, parents
who have instilled in them the Christian virtues will
find them a ready source of companionship and comfort.
Sad indeed is the aging husband or wife who has lost his
or her mate and must now face the remaining years without the solace of loving children. But blessed indeed is the
widow or widower who is fully welcomed, cared for,
and comforted by his loving children as they express their
appreciation for the care that he with his mate gave them
in childhood. Neither riches, nor a successful career,
nor any other accomplishment in life can compare with
the sense of joy that can be his in knowing that he has his
own loving children who care for him in his waning years
of life.

In view of the undeniable advantages of the large
Christian family, procreated and educated with the love
of God and in the light of Our Lord's teachings, why does
there exist such a consistent campaign against it? This
campaign is not a myth. It is evidenced by those who invariably regard the mother of five or more children as
being exploited and overworked, even as the victim of her
own husband's unbridled passion. It is evidenced also by
the expressions of sympathy that come from some persons when they hear of families with seven or eight children. It is also evidenced by the commonly heard expressions of others that the father and mother of a large

number of children should "learn about birth control."

This campaign against large families rarely comes from men and women who have dedicated themselves to the ideal of Christian family life. Instead, it generally comes from men and women who have perhaps one or two, or perhaps none. It is a campaign conducted out of ignorance—not from a real knowledge of the sense of security, love, and affection which can be developed in the large family where parents and children are united in making their home a Christian chapel.

Those who look down upon the large family generally consider the amount of hard work by the parents that may be involved in supporting it and at the sacrifices that all must make. They see the father's shoes which need repair and note that the mother's dress is of an old style and not cut in the latest design. They see a younger child wearing the sweater worn by his older brothers when they were his size, and they observe that the children lack toys bought at the store but instead must suffer the "trauma" of playing with things they have made themselves.

Surely no one can deny that the mother and father of a large family have difficult jobs requiring much hard work, prayer, and patience. There are doubtless moments when the parents succumb to moods of depression and wonder whether their sacrifices are worth while. There may even be moments when they might think that the prophets of the one-child or two-child family may be right. But such moments quickly pass.

Dedicated Christian parents of large families realize that the satisfaction they get is the most rewarding experience they can have—more rewarding than anything

that might have come to them if they had succumbed to
the temptation to limit their offspring to one or two.
They realize that the lasting joys in life come not from
pleasure, not from the possession of material things, nor
from the "easy life" in which comfort is all important,
but rather in the satisfaction of doing a job which must
be done because that is what Almighty God wants them
to do.

OLDER PEOPLE KNOW ADVANTAGES
OF PARENTHOOD

The "moment of truth" in this question often arrives
when parents reach their forties and realize that the wife
is at the end of her childbearing years, and will no longer
be able to have a baby. At this point, it is not unusual for
a man and woman to look back upon their years of marriage and to wonder whether they had acted wisely in
having the number of children they have. It is the rare
couple who believe that they had too many. Rather, most
wish that they had had more.

Not untypical was the attitude of a Catholic mother on
the day the last of her fourteen children trotted off to
her first day in school. A neighbor commented: "This
must be a happy day for you. Now you can feel free at
last." The mother wiped a few tears from her eyes and
said:

"It is one of the saddest days of my life. Do you realize
I will never again hold a baby of my own in my arms?"

In the same vein, a radio announcer recently interviewed a woman, a mother of nineteen children. After

expressing amazement, he asked her if she would have as large a family if she had the opportunity to live her life over. She hesitated but a moment and then answered, "Yes, for I can't think of one child I'd do without."

The advantages of parenthood often can be realized most fully by talking with old couples who are childless, or have one or two children. Of course, God plays an important part in procreation. Men and women who are willing and even anxious to perform their responsibilities as parents may be denied the opportunity. Perhaps the wife has had a difficult time carrying a fetus to the normal length of pregnancy. Perhaps one or the other may have been unable to play his or her part in conceiving a new life. There may have been other circumstances beyond their control. Such persons can console themselves with the thought that they were willing to become parents, and their inability to do so does not reflect upon them morally. Thus they have this comfort despite the natural sadness they may feel at their inability to have children of their own.

But it is those who could have had children and for selfish reasons refused to do so, who feel the loss most bitterly. For it is true that a husband does not achieve the full dimensions of his manhood unless he achieves fatherhood, and that the true fulfillment for a wife comes only when she experiences the feeling of partnership with God in the creation of life.

It is parents who experience one of the greatest of all joys—the unquestioning love of a child. And the couple who deliberately and selfishly avoided children will go to their graves with the thought that they leave no one behind to carry on for them. When one sees such as these in their old age they are often the disappointed, the frustrated, the embittered, for they realize that for no other reason but their own selfish decision, they have missed one of the great experiences which God has offered to mankind.

TWO BASIC PRINCIPLES

To sum up, then, any discussion of family limitation by a Catholic couple must be based on these two premises:

1. God created marriage as His means of propagating mankind. A Catholic may choose to marry or not to marry, but once he decides to marry, he must be willing to do the work which this vocation entails. Thus, the Catholic bride and bridegroom must be willing to become parents if God chooses to bless their union with children.

2. The family with many children, in which God has the place of honor, is an object of Christian admiration. There may be reasons why Catholic couples decide not to have children for short periods, or even for the duration of their marriage. But this does not alter the fact that large families are, in the words of Pope Pius XII:

"Those blessed by God, beloved by the Church, and considered by it as one of its most precious treasures."

2.

What Christian Parenthood
Does *not* Mean

ONE distortion of the Church's teaching on marriage
should be cleared up right away. She does not say: "Have
all the babies you can."

A Christian couple do not fulfill their responsibilities to
God simply by engaging in the process of intercourse
willy-nilly and without concern for the birth that may
result. They do not do their duty simply by having babies. The first purpose of marriage is the procreation *and*
education of children. Couples, therefore, fulfill their responsibilities only when they strive to educate their children to lead worthy lives and ultimately gain the sight of
God in Heaven. Something of the importance of this
work may be measured by the fact that the act of conception takes but seconds; that pregnancy takes months;
but that the education of the child requires years. In one
sense the later years are more creative than the first seconds.

Christian parenthood, therefore, can never be merely

biological. Truly Christian parents are those who accept a child as a sacred gift from God, and who fully recognize the advantages that children can mean for their own personal spiritual development. They also have a sufficient respect for parenthood so that they do not jump into marriage without taking careful account of the duties of this state in life and their ability to fulfill them. They do not undertake procreation without pondering the obligation which they must assume to give their children an upbringing that will enable them to use the talents which God gives them, and most importantly, to save their souls.

Christian parents fully recognize the tremendous privilege and commitment which bringing a child into the world involves. And because of this, they are made humble and prudent about their obligations to do their work of parenthood so that the child can return to God at the end of his days. For this very reason, therefore, Christian parenthood is always careful, loving, and responsible parenthood.

This important truth is often overlooked by persons outside the Church who thoughtlessly charge that the Church is merely interested in "numbers" and requires a couple to have as many children as they can squeeze into their childbearing years. This belief—absurd as it is—is often held even by some inside the Church.

Not long ago, I observed a man and his wife on the street. The man was stumbling behind a baby carriage and a few dirty children straggled on behind. The husband was drunk again and, this being the middle of a weekday, it was also obvious that he was again unemployed. I noticed that the couple had with them only a few of their children. Of the older offspring who were not present, one was a mental case, another had become addicted to drugs, and the others were continually involved in serious scrapes in the neighborhood. All that kept the family together was the charity of the pastor and the monthly check from the despairing relief agency in the city.

When I saw the parents, I tried to remind them that they had gone beyond the point at which prudence and moderation suggested that they avoid bringing into the world other children who would face desperately long odds in such an environment. With a righteous toss of the head, the husband remarked that in having children, he and his wife were only doing what the Church wanted.

This is a typical example of the cases cited by advocates of contraception to "support" their argument that the Church does not care for the welfare of children, but is concerned with getting as many born as possible (in order to swell the ranks of Catholics, increase their political influence, etc.). Unfortunately, there are similar examples of men and women who breed heedlessly and leave their children without any moral standard to guide them as they grope through life. These cases are sad indeed. But no one is more saddened than the Church by the spectacle of an innocent child in a home from which all virtue has fled, and in which he is virtually doomed to spiritual, emotional, and even physical misery.

A PARENT'S ULTIMATE RESPONSIBILITY

The Church has always taught that a human being's destiny is heaven. One of the first principles a child learns in his catechism is that God made him to know Him, love Him, and serve Him in this world in order to be happy with Him in the next. The Church also stresses that a child can best learn to know God through the teachings and example of his parents. She has always upheld the right and duty of parents to serve as the child's first teacher, and through the centuries, she has always resisted attempts by the state to take that right from them.

The doctrines of the Church reinforce the basic obligation of parents to serve as good examples for their children. For example, she teaches that marriage must be for life and is an instrument of love and fidelity—a teaching which requires parents to work together in creating a home atmosphere in which a child can reach his full spiritual and emotional development. The Church also has always stressed the importance of choosing a marriage partner who will sanctify the other and help in the achievement of his or her eternal destiny. This choice of a suitable marriage partner is, of course, a first requisite for the proper upbringing of children.

In taking her stands on the great moral and social problems of the present day, the Church also reinforces the duty of parents to provide the best possible atmosphere for their children. In fighting against divorce, she stresses the importance to the child of continuous care by both parents. In resisting trends towards teen-age marriages, she emphasizes the importance of a mature approach towards this sacrament and urges young men and women to wait until they are ready to perform the duties of parenthood in a responsible way. In opposing the many signs of unbridled sexual freedom wherever they appear, she is fighting to uphold the dignity of the act of procreation and the dignity of the child who results from that act. In upholding the dignity of the large family, she encourages parents to give each child the greatest possible welcome into the world—the feeling that he is wanted and loved.

Any child is worthy of a loving welcome into the world, and is entitled to understanding, acceptance, and true guidance throughout his formative years. He deserves this in his own right, as one who must some day stand before the judgment seat of God and will be helped or hindered in achieving his goals in life by the teaching of his parents.

Each child is also important as the parent's own contact with generations yet unborn. He will carry the torch given him to the generation that follows him, and the light cast by that torch will reflect the father's and mother's character long after they are gone. It will help light the way to his salvation—and to the salvation of generations yet unborn.

On the other hand, how often can we trace the evil-doers of today—the criminals, public sinners, the scoffers at morality and even at God Himself—to parents, grandparents, even great-grandparents who obviously fulfilled the function of procreation but who failed completely in their task of educating their children to live creditable lives in the sight of the Creator.

The ideal of Christian parenthood, therefore, never has been to engage in a race for babies without regard for the consequences. It is not the having of babies that is important in itself; it is the having of children to whom you will give sufficient training and example to enable them to make use of the talents which God gives them in a way which serves God and man.

CHILDREN HELP CHILDREN

It is in the light of these teachings that the Church sees the large family, motivated by Christian principles, as the one which gives a child the best opportunity of achieving his eternal destiny. For it has been her experience over the centuries—and the experience of society in general—that the one-child family is a seedbed for selfishness. The individual child becomes the focus of his parents' attention. He soon learns that he can receive what he wants almost habitually and he never learns the importance of giving as well as taking. He is denied the valuable training of being required to deal with those older and younger than himself. He frequently fails to learn the importance of submitting to authority and the equal importance of displaying charity and generosity towards those younger and weaker than himself. It is often the case, therefore, that the "only child"—or the child in a two-child or three-child family where births are spaced so widely apart that for all purposes in his upbringing, each child is an "only child"—is less privileged and receives less actual training for the give-and-take of life, than the child with half a dozen brothers and sisters.

Of themselves, mere numbers tell little about how well a couple fulfill the obligations of parenthood. As we have noted, the husband and wife who are childless through no desire of their own may be leading more pleasing lives in the sight of God than the couple who fulfill to over-flowing the obligation to have children, but who fail to give them the upbringing they need to lead good Christian lives. On the other hand, simply because a couple have but two or three children does not mean that they are truly "responsible parents."

One couple had two children, a boy and a girl, neatly spaced four years apart. Here was an "ideal family unit" in the eyes of many moderns. The father was a prominent executive in a large corporation, and his wife played an active part in social affairs of their community. Readers of the society pages could often see pictures of them, impeccably attired, as they attended the most glittering social functions and important civic affairs of the community.

While the husband was busy making a name for himself in business, and the wife was achieving equal prominence in the social world, they were miserable parents. From birth, the children were turned over to paid nurses and maids. Sometimes days passed when the youngsters saw neither mother nor father. Although they lived in the most luxurious surroundings, and had all the material comforts anyone could ask, the children were virtually orphans.

Even before they completed their elementary school education, they were hustled off to boarding school. There the daughter got into a scrape with an older boy and was threatened with expulsion. She found it necessary to write a note to her father, asking for an appointment to see him. Unfortunately, he had many important conferences to attend on the day that she sought to see him, and could not meet her.

Is it any wonder that the girl is now, at twenty-two years of age, already a divorcee and has acquired an unsavory reputation as a person devoid of moral scruples who has apparently made it her career to have affairs with married men with the seeming intent of breaking up their marriages? Her brother equally lacks moral character. He is a "playboy" to whom adultery and alcoholism seem to come naturally. The parents of the two children sometimes wonder why their two youngsters have gone wrong. Didn't the parents limit their number of offspring to a number that society finds acceptable? Didn't they provide luxurious comforts for their youngsters and expend thousands of dollars every year on their schooling? They have still been unable to realize that they neglected to give the one thing which is truly necessary for the proper spiritual and emotional development of any child. They neglected to give their own time, concern, and attention.

By contrast, there was a family living in a much poorer part of town, in a large house which had seen much better days. It was not the kind of house that would appear on the pages of a home-and-garden magazine. In the front lawn you could find many spots of hard dirt where grass could not possibly grow because it had been beaten down by the feet of youngsters playing baseball. In the back yard were similar bare patches all around an obviously homemade basketball net. As you enter the living room, you could not help but notice the age of the furniture, and the fact that toys were scattered about the floor. In the bedroom there were bunk beds and just enough cubic air space for breathing. According to some standards, the children brought to life in such a home were unprivileged, because they lacked modern equipment to play with, and often had to use last year's clothing and last year's toys. Even worse from the modern point of view, they were often obliged to do without little comforts and luxuries they might have liked to have.

There were seven children in this family, and the mother struggled to maintain the home and to feed and clothe the children on a postman's salary. Sometimes she had difficulty in doing so. The better cuts of meat were a complete stranger to this home, but the presence of a huge pot of beef or lamb stew was more familiar—and the children did not seem to mind.

Lacking money for the movies and such things, the family had to make their recreation. They had an ancient upright piano which came from the mother's parents, and many an evening after the children washed the dishes, she played old songs while the father and children sang.

These parents were not "absentee parents." Each evening, the father reviewed the events of the day with his family, correcting those who had made mistakes, rejoicing in the triumphs each had experienced, and consoling each in his defeats. It was an inspiring sight to the entire parish to see the father and mother as they walked to the altar rail with all their children to receive the Holy Eucharist.

This was a family in which goodness was truly cemented by the interest, concern, and example of the parents. And the results achieved truly reflect the home life.

Of the seven, one is now completing his studies in the seminary; another is a schoolteacher; a third, a member of the police force. Two are attending college on scholarships they won through their own efforts and their parents' encouragement. The other two are in high school —both a wonderful example of good conduct, who reflect full credit upon their parents.

Underprivileged? By the world's standards, perhaps they were. But they were so busy enjoying the love and warmth of Christian family life that they never knew it. And they will never believe that they were. For each child has received a greater heritage than any material wealth can provide.

A SENSE OF VALUES

No one need look far to find striking examples of parents who have successfully raised large families with small resources. Dwight D. Eisenhower was one of seven children in a modest-income family. The greatest of composers, Beethoven, was one of eleven; the American hero of World War I, General Pershing, one of eleven; the great and recently canonized Saint Mother Cabrini was one of thirteen. Many of the greatest men in all history— men like Michelangelo and Leonardo da Vinci and Benjamin Franklin—were born into poor families whose parents, fortunately, had never heard of contraceptives.

We can also observe countless examples in our own society. There is the schoolteacher and his wife who have brought nine children up on his very limited income— each one a college graduate, including two doctors.

There is a farmer with thirteen children, among them a priest, two nuns, a college professor, a librarian. And there is also the immigrant who has worked with his hands all his life, but with his wife has managed to raise twelve children. None of them has completed college, but every one is a hard-working, responsible citizen—a greater asset to the community than some persons with several degrees but no morality.

Some moderns express the viewpoint that there is "something indecent" about a large family. Recently, a man and wife with six children attended a neighborhood party and met another couple of the same age who were childless. When the parents left the party in order to get the baby-sitter back to her home at the specified hour, the childless wife turned to the group remaining and said she felt nothing but sympathy for a woman who was "tied down" with so many children. "Hasn't she heard about birth control?" the childless woman asked. "Somebody should send a representative from 'Planned Parenthood' to see her."

The remark got back to the mother of six, as such remarks usually do. The mother thought for a moment, and then commented: "Since I'm the one with the children, I'm probably in a better position to say whether anyone should feel sorry for me. And I certainly don't feel sorry for myself. In fact, I have no sorrow left after the amount I feel for someone without even one child."

MODERN PROBLEMS

In upholding the ideal of the large family, we must be realistic enough to recognize that it is considerably more difficult for the average Catholic couple of today to have as many children as parents of earlier generations brought into the world. For the modern couple must decide how to fulfill the responsibilities of marriage under conditions entirely different from those which prevailed in earlier times.

For example, for the first time in history, men and women can exercise a reasonably accurate choice over whether or not they will become parents. Only in these times have we scientific knowledge of the workings of a woman's cycle so that we can predict the days in which she is sterile—not capable of conceiving children, and days in which she is fertile—when intercourse is likely to result in conception. Therefore, men and women for the first time can exercise a deliberate choice as to whether their act of marital love will result in pregnancy. In earlier times, couples lacked the precise knowledge available today, and could not be sure whether intercourse at any particular time would or would not lead to the creation of life.

Moreover, modern society is questioning the purposes of marriage to an extent unknown in Christian history. The growth of the contraceptive mentality, coupled with an almost insane preoccupation with sexual gratification, has caused millions of persons outside the Church, and, unfortunately, some within it, to argue that personal happiness should be a couple's first concern, and that they should not consider themselves obliged to have children. This view of marriage as an instrument for recreation and not procreation has spread throughout the Western world with the result that men and women are coming to regard marriage as a private affair which involves no obligations to society and can be entered and left as the whim moves them.

It is true that a second purpose of the marital act (and second not because of its own unimportance but because of that which comes first) is the opportunity it affords the husband and wife to express their love for each other. The giving of one's self in the act of sex is both a fruit of love and a source of love—and as such it serves the high purpose of strengthening the bond that exists between man and wife. The act of intercourse is rightly performed with the intention of achieving a fuller union of mind and heart of the couple involved. But this rich joy takes on true value only when it pours forth on the children begotten of that love.

A third factor which makes the problems of the modern married couple unique is that the social pressures against the large family are perhaps greater than ever before. Quite often, in modern life, it constitutes an act of sheer heroism for a man and woman to have several children. We shall examine these pressures at greater length in the next chapter, but for the moment let us observe that some of these pressures are the result of modern influences, some derive from the very nature of our industrial society, and some stem from the "emancipation" of women.

In the face of these factors, a Catholic couple often need a powerful sense of dedication to the work of their marriage. They must clearly understand why God has called them to their vocation, and they must be prepared to stand alone if necessary in the face of the disinterest or hostility of their neighbors. And often, to a greater extent perhaps than ever before, a devoted Catholic couple must prayerfully ask themselves whether it is wise for them to have additional children or whether the exercise of their God-given prudence suggests that they cannot reasonably bring another child into the world at this time and provide him with the essentials he needs for the development of his personality, the achievement of a dignified place in society as an adult, and ultimately a place in Heaven.

In asking this question, they must determine whether they are able not only to fulfill the physical process of giving birth to a healthy child, but also whether they will be able to care properly for him through all the years of his upbringing and dependency. In answering it, they will first draw upon their understanding of why they were called to the married state. They will recognize that the couple who do not choose to have a family are the exception, not the rule. They will use their God-given reason to determine whether they can indeed perform all of the functions of father and mother who are devoted to the care, welfare, and progress of their children. They will be aware of the pressures exerted upon them on all sides to restrict the number of their children. They will honestly strive to determine whether they must bow to those pressures because of their inability to overcome them, or whether they are pressures they should rightfully ignore.

Above all, they will not overlook the fact that a child is conceived only when God wills it. The Providence of the Creator is perhaps the most important factor a couple will consider when deciding whether to have another baby. They will never forget that God rewards those who trust Him as they do His work—that, in the words of the old Portuguese saying, "every child is born with a loaf of bread under his arm." Or, as Pope Pius XII stated in an address he gave to the Association of Large Families of Rome and Italy, "faith in God supplies parents with the strength necessary to face the sacrifices and renunciations required for the rearing of children." The couple will also remember these words which the priest delivers before the marriage ceremony: "If true love and the unselfish spirit of perfect sacrifice guides your every action, you can expect the greatest measure of earthly happiness that may be allotted to man in this vale of tears."

FOUR CLASSES OF PARENTS

In arriving at their own free decision as to whether they can prudently provide for a child, a husband and wife will put themselves into one of four categories. In one category are the truly *irresponsible*—those unwilling to respond to the call of the vocation they have entered, who are unwilling to have children at all, or who are indifferent about having them but are unwilling to do the work of educating them. In this group are those to whom God has given all that any person needs for parenthood, but who for their own selfish reasons refuse to make the sacrifice. And there are also those who refuse to heed the common sense which tells them they are not equipped to give a new child what he needs in a material or spiritual sense for his proper development as a child of God.

In a second category are the *timid*—those who are excessively fearful of the future, excessively lacking in confidence that they could carry the normal burdens of parenthood. People such as these have our sympathy, however mistaken they may be in their outlook.

In the third group are the *dutiful,* those Christians who, after prayerfully considering the pros and cons of having a child, do what is expected of them. They do not volunteer above and beyond the normal call of duty, but rather are like the soldiers who will do what they must—and therefore merit praise for living up to the requirements of their profession.

In the fourth—and select category—are the *heroic*—those who recognize that many sacrifices (and perhaps great ones) will be involved in their decision for parenthood, but they proceed nonetheless to have their children, and to give them the loving care and direction which are their rightful due. These men and women are imbued with an exalted concept of Christian marriage and a desire to live it in accord with its highest ideals. These are the admirable ones—for among them are numbered those who in ancient times would have stood up to their persecutors and died, if need be, on behalf of the faith that was in them.

3.

The Problems of
Married People

ALWAYS holding high the ideal of the large family as the
best medium by which parents and children can save
their souls and gain "the greatest measure of earthly happiness that may be allotted to man in this vale of tears,
the Church nevertheless recognizes that truly devoted
Catholic couples may be forced to limit the number of
their children. As Pope Pius XII stated in 1951, in an
address to the Family Association of Italy, "The Church
can sympathize with and understand the very real difficulties connected with married life in our time."

It would be unrealistic to overlook the difficulties
facing parents which result from the conditions of modern
life. Nor would it be realistic to assume that to have and
to educate properly a large family, a couple need only
the will to do so.

Unfortunately, the Catholic husband and wife seeking to fulfill their vocation are beset by pressures from
all directions that make it difficult, if not often impossible,

to have a family of the size that was common a few generations ago. These pressures spring from the nature of modern society—the tendency of men and women to group together in large cities, the growth of huge corporations and a class of wage earners who are totally dependent upon their salary and often unsure of their ability to support children. The pressures result from the increased financial cost of having children—of paying doctors and hospitals when bringing them into the world, of feeding, clothing, and educating them. Then, too, the modern individual has increased standards of expectation—a desire for more of the material comforts of life. He often views the new infant as a threat to the realization of these standards.

The tendency away from frequent childbearing results in part from the changed position of women in modern life. Many wives no longer are content to remain in the home and fulfill their traditional functions as mothers and homemakers.

And perhaps the strongest influence of all is the secularization of the world, with its incessant emphasis on "personal fulfillment" and its demands that men and women get rid of any responsibility that causes inconvenience or hardship.

Some of these influences—such as the development of mass-production industries—may be good in themselves, and may have the general effect of improving man's living standards and erasing social injustices. But they also have a secondary effect which makes Christian family life difficult to achieve.

Let us examine the most important pressures in greater detail.

The pressures of industrialization. We live in an industrial society. Innumerable machines do work which was formerly done by hand. In our time, the huge corporation with thousands—and sometimes hundreds of thousands—of employees, is commonplace. Vast factories and office buildings, gigantic stores, service organizations, and enterprises of all kinds, can be seen almost everywhere. Fewer and fewer men and women obtain their living from farms or in small villages as craftsmen and small shopkeepers, as was the rule a few generations ago. In Western societies, more and more heads of families are compensated for their work in the form of wages at the end of a week or month.

This is in marked contrast to the conditions under which our grandfathers lived. In their time, most people were closer to the land. They enjoyed a basic security because they lived in homes, however humble, which would not be taken from them, and they depended upon very simple things to satisfy their basic needs. They generally were confident that they would not go hungry— even in times of scarcity—because there were usually some crops in the field to sustain them. They were largely self-sufficient. They made the clothes they wore, built the homes they lived in, made the bread they ate. Because they had a greater sense of self-reliance, a greater expectation that the necessities of life could be obtained, and because their own living standards were low, they brought large numbers of children into the world without fears that the increased numbers would drastically lower their levels. In those times, a baby cost little in monetary terms.

For all the material comforts and high living stand-

ards he enjoys, the modern wage earner often lacks the
security his grandfather knew. Dependent upon his
weekly wage, he will suffer acutely if economic conditions
cause unemployment, if his employer decides to dispense
with his services, if his union undertakes a costly strike
for better living conditions. Moreover, today's typical
wage earner depends upon money to buy the things
which older generations made for themselves. Instead of
building his own home, he pays to have one built for him.
Even if he ventures to build it himself, he must pay for expensive materials—plumbing equipment, electrical wiring,
and the like. In any event, it is quite likely that he will
not truly own it until he has paid off a bank loan with
wages earned over a period of twenty or thirty years. If
his children lack clothing, his wife probably is not
equipped by training or desire to make it. The clothes—
or at least the basic cloth—must be bought at the store.
If the family needs food, there usually is no convenient
field near by upon which crops can be grown. Unless it
has money to buy groceries, it will go hungry.

A modern man and woman, tied as they are to the
weekly paycheck, are likely to think more seriously about
the responsibility of providing for a child than would a
couple in earlier times who could be fairly confident that
their youngster would have enough food, clothing, and
shelter until he could support himself.

Until the present century, it usually could be safely
predicted that a child would live all his days and finally
die in or near the same community in which he first saw
light. Families often could trace back to their forefathers
who lived in the very same community. It was not unlikely for a child to be born into the very home in which

his great-grandparents had been born. And surrounding the child would be not only his own parents, but grandmothers and grandfathers, aunts and uncles, cousins, friends, and neighbors who knew the parents from childhood. There was a true family spirit, and it was traditional for one family member to help another in time of need.

This meant that the mother-to-be could surely receive help from her relatives or friends. Someone would be there if she encountered difficulties during her pregnancy, to help her during her delivery, and to care afterwards for mother and infant. From one relative might come clothing for the baby, perhaps garments another child had outgrown. From another might come a crib; from a third, warm blankets. If the child became sick, the older members of the family would not be at a loss over what to do. And in the rare event that the parents of the new child wished to leave their home for an evening, relatives or friends too could always be found to take care of the child while they were gone. There was a complete sense of family unity, and little reason therefore to regard childbirth as a great economic or emotional burden upon the parents.

Conditions today are almost the complete reverse. Increasing numbers of persons live in communities many miles from where their parents lived, and perhaps thousands of miles from where their grandparents were born. As a result of the development of the automobile, other fast methods of transportation, and the wide dispersion of industry, it is not a novelty to see a man raise his family thousands of miles from where his brothers and sisters are living.

In one typical case, a husband and wife were brought

up within the same block in New York City—the very block in which lived four uncles and aunts and more than twenty cousins. This man and woman had six children. Not one child lives on the same block today. One, a soldier, is stationed in Turkey. Another works in an airplane factory in Los Angeles. A third works for a large corporation, and within the past ten years has been transferred from Detroit to Fort Worth to Buffalo, New York. Another works for the Federal government in Washington. Only two of the six still live in the New York area— but so far from each other that it takes two hours to go from the home of one to the other, with the result that the trip is made only a few times a year.

Needless to say, each of these children must depend upon himself or herself exclusively for the aid which in other times would have been provided by relatives or friends. When they anticipate the birth of a child, they must consider what it will cost for medical care, for clothing and other equipment for the baby, possibly for a nurse to help the mother after her return from the hospital, and for many other things which their parents, uncles, and aunts did for each other without charge.

In earlier times, parents were unfamiliar with much of what we know about sanitation and health, and they stoically accepted the difficulties that sometimes attended the birth of a child. The changes that have taken place in medical care in the present century have been truly phenomenal. Sixty years ago, the typical baby was born at home, perhaps with a midwife in attendance, perhaps —if the family had very high standards of living—with a doctor. There was little knowledge of what could be done to insure safety in childbirth, and prenatal care was the exception rather than the rule. Likewise, the "pediatrician," the doctor who cares exclusively for newborn babies and young children, was virtually unknown. As a result, of course, mortality rates for mothers and infants were staggeringly higher than they are now. Today, all that has changed. The woman who goes to a doctor as soon as she realizes she is pregnant, who follows his advice all the time she is carrying the baby, and who delivers her child in a hospital, is almost certain to come through the experience with both herself and child in a healthy condition.

This is a notable forward step in the story of mankind. But it makes having a child much more costly than was true in 1900. A couple seeking adequate medical care before, during, and after childbirth must count on spending perhaps as much money as a husband earns in a whole month.

In older societies, a child was considered a success if he became the same sort of man as his father, and did the same kind of work. A child was not made to feel that he had failed if he did not exceed his father's performance and did not raise his standard of living during his lifetime. Today, of course, a child expects to outperform his parents. Many social commentators say that the modern bride and bridegroom expect to begin life with a standard of living that their parents enjoyed after working and saving for twenty-five years.

At any rate, a typical parent now tries to give his youngster a higher level of education than he himself received. This has even become an economic necessity. The child born in 1900 who received only an elementary-school education had fair prospects of earning a living that would enable him to support a family in reasonable comfort. The child born in 1930 would need several years of secondary-school education, if not a diploma, to qualify for the same type of position. As of today, with the increasing emphasis upon technological training, a secondary-school diploma is a minimum necessity, and a degree from a college or university is virtually required if anyone seeks to rise to a position of prestige in the community.

Economists have repeatedly warned that the youngster who leaves school today before obtaining at least a high school diploma will be increasingly at a disadvantage in seeking employment because the demand for specialists in all types of work will make it less and less possible for the uneducated person to fit into the employment picture. This trend has already begun in the United States, where the number of unemployed unskilled workers has risen constantly in the midst of the greatest prosperity the world has ever known. Parents, therefore, are justified in wanting to enable their children to make full use of the talents which God has given them. Unfortunately, however, costs of education have risen consistently. It has been estimated that by 1975 the cost of attending a university will be 50 per cent greater than it is today. And with so many husbands continuing their schooling after marriage, fatherhood becomes truly expensive.

When most people lived on farms or in small communities, parents often had economic reasons for wanting children. A child on the farm could milk the cows, plant seed, harvest crops, and do other chores as well as adults. (The custom of giving summer vacations to school children resulted from the fact that their parents wanted them to work on the farms during those months.) Before and after attending his classes, a farm youngster seven years old could often do enough work to pay the cost of supporting him. In the towns, children also used to begin working at an early age—perhaps even as young as ten years—and the wages they earned often were sufficient to pay for their meager food and shelter.

Economic reasons for wanting children are virtually nonexistent today. While farm children can generally do much to help their parents, much of the work is now done by mechanics who are trained to operate heavy machinery such as tractors and crop-pickers. As for paid employment outside the home, in most places it is forbidden to hire young children. Therefore, the parents must support them entirely until they reach young manhood or young womanhood.

When the modern boy becomes eighteen, he may enter a college or university and is likely to be supported by his parents at least in part. Even if he pays his own way, he will probably be unable to contribute anything to the family. He may be called to duty with the Army, in which case he will also be unable to make any substantial contribution to the family. At the end of his college or Army career, he is usually ready to marry. As a result, he may never contribute anything to his parents. On the other hand, the cost of bringing him to the age of marriage may total as much as twenty thousand dollars.

Even when a modern couple are heroically disposed to bring a large number of children into the world, they will often find no place to live in dignity. In other times, when the large family was an accepted part of society, it was relatively easy to obtain living space for children. If a family lived on a farm, for example, extra rooms would be built if needed. In towns and cities, houses were made with a large number of bedrooms to accommodate the large families which were customary. Moreover, older generations did not think twice about putting several children to sleep in the same room, if not the same bed. The landlord who posted a "no children wanted" sign on his property would soon discover himself with no tenants at all.

Today, however, houses and apartments seem to be built for the "ideal" family of three children or less. A newspaperman in New York City with seven children scoured the length and breadth of that city trying to find suitable living quarters for his family at a price he could pay. On the few occasions when he discovered an apartment large enough, he also discovered that the owner completely lost interest in renting it upon learning of the number of children involved. This man was finally forced to rent two connecting apartments in a building in which the owner consented to let him live—but at a price much greater than he could actually afford. Other heads of families who seek to buy new houses for large numbers of youngsters often find it difficult to obtain one with more than three bedrooms at a reasonable price. Parents of large families may often discover—even if they can afford plenty of space—that they may be obliged to rent apartments in a run-down section, or to buy older houses which have adequate space but lack modern conveniences that other couples take for granted.

Among the benefits wrought by our industrial society, there has been the benefit of increased leisure time and a greater amount of worldly goods for the average person. Unlike the husband and father of earlier generations, who left his home at dawn and returned after dusk and enjoyed one day of rest a week, the modern employee probably works no more than forty-five hours each week, and possibly even less. And many union leaders now speak of such things as a seven-hour working day, and a four-day working week.

Thanks to this shorter work week, the typical husband has more leisure time than ever. However, the woman of the house is hardly disposed to watch idly as her husband relaxes while she works at the routine tasks of child-caring and homemaking. As she observes her husband with free evenings and weekends to watch television and engage in other recreational activities, she rightfully wishes to be his companion. Obviously, if she has a large number of children—involving long periods of pregnancy, periods when she is tied down in caring for the young baby, and periods when she must devote herself to looking after a number of young children—she has little opportunity to enjoy her husband's leisure time with him. As a result, some wives think that it is unfair to be "tied down" by many children and to have little leisure time when their husbands have so much.

Another benefit of the machine age—the making available to average men and women of material comforts unheard of by kings a century ago—has also affected modern attitudes towards large families. In the days before radio, television, and other mass media, most persons lived in tightly knit communities and had little contact with the outside world. They lived and died as did their parents—often in the same house, using the same beds, tables and chairs, the same tools for farming and cooking that their forebears had used. They had little in a material sense, but were able to live reasonably dignified lives with the little that they had. What was more important for their serenity was that they expected little else. They did not feel deprived because they did not have a car, a clothes washer, a TV set, or stereo hi-fi phonograph.

Few such isolated places remain in the Western world. There are few areas where radio is unknown (and few, in fact, where television aerials do not sprout from the rooftops) and few areas which do not have newspapers delivered to their doorstep. All over North America and Europe, even low-paid workers aspire to the ownership of a motor bicycle, if not an automobile, to have several suits in their closets, and to have labor-saving devices like vacuum cleaners to do some of the tedious work that formerly was done by hand. The placing of such possessions within reach of the average person has resulted in what has been called the "revolution of expectations." The common people of the world see that it is possible to lead a comfortable existence with labor-saving devices, adequate clothing, food, shelter, and other recreational devices. And they want to do so.

No longer are they satisfied to live as their parents did. No longer are they resigned to working from dawn to dusk for life's bare necessities. But often, in order to gain these comforts, the average man and woman must choose between the material goods of life and children. How will the average couple decide to use their money? Will they spend it on a baby or a television set? Which do they want more—a new car or a new child?

As they strive to reach a decision, they are bombarded on all sides by advertising which urges them to seek their happiness in material goods. It has been said that modern man was born not to serve God, but rather to serve as a consumer for industry. Billions are spent on advertising to make him a consumer of things—to encourage him to buy a new automobile, new household appliances, equipment to beautify face and figure, gadgets for the home.

The modern husband and wife are constantly besieged from morning to night with pressures to spend their available funds on the products of industry. They will look in vain for advertisements urging them to use their funds to procreate and educate children.

With this development of a society that places its emphasis on money and the things that money will buy, the symbols of success have undergone a significant change—a change which also puts at a disadvantage the husband and wife seeking to fulfill their obligations of parenthood. In previous generations, one could enter any community and would know, without being told, who the people of prestige were. They were the village priest, the family doctor, the schoolteacher, the policeman. They were judged by the positions they held and the services they performed. No one asked their salary. They were honored for their position and achievements. Similarly, the husband and wife with a large family were regarded with respect, even if they sometimes found it difficult to make ends meet. The man with many children was often considered a success, and the amount he earned was of secondary importance.

Today, however, the symbol of success is almost invariably the possession and display of wealth. The position that a man holds—and the quality of the work he does—is of minor importance, unless he receives an income which clearly establishes that he is indeed an important person. The author who writes a book, the scientist who does a piece of research, the playwright who produces a play, the artist who paints pictures, need worry less about the quality of his work than about the quantity of money it earns. If a book is a best seller or a play is performed before capacity audiences, its producers need not worry whether it has any moral value or whether it even has a corrupting influence. It makes money; therefore is successful. A remark quoted approvingly in these times was made by a highly paid entertainer whose work had been widely criticized. "I cried all the way to the bank," he said.

Emphasis upon money as the symbol of success means that the man who earns a low salary—regardless of his work—is looked down upon. For example, the shortage of teachers results from the fact that they are poorly paid and lack prestige; therefore no longer does teaching attract young people. A teacher sometimes earns as little as a factory worker, and in modern society he does not have much greater standing in the community.

Since the man who has money and uses it to acquire things, carries the greatest prestige in modern life, it is perhaps natural that socially ambitious couples will spend their money on things which raise their stature in their neighbors' eyes. Thus it is the big car, the new house, the most fashionable clothing, which establishes that a person is successful. On the other hand, the parents of a large family are likely to be considered unsuccessful, because in order to have children they probably have sacrificed some of the more glittering luxuries. In the modern world, the prestige-hungry couple can achieve a higher status if they have one child who can be given the most expensive clothing and toys, rather than several children who may have to wear less fashionable garments and to use secondhand playthings.

The changed status of women. This is another fundamental factor which makes it difficult for conscientious Catholic couples to achieve the ideal of a large family. These changes, also a world-wide trend, have been going on also since the turn of the century. They have freed women from their old bondage and have produced many benefits by eliminating many abuses which gave women an inferior status and made them "second-class citizens." Beneficial as this movement has been in general, it has had a secondary result of changing the traditional attitudes which women have always held toward the importance of home and children.

As one example: The fight for suffrage in the United States was led by women who, perhaps to make their arguments more forcible, adopted extreme positions. Many argued that women should rise up against men who were striving to turn them into "maternity machines." These feminists often argued that in having babies women had been denied the right to develop their full personalities.

Some of this extreme point of view survives. There are women who argue that the wife who has babies forges a chain around her neck and becomes a slave in bondage. Needless to say, the attitude that a wife who has several children is inferior to one who is childless or has one or two, is a new one in human history. Instead of being regarded as the noblest work that a woman can perform,

the procreation and education of the young is regarded—
in a few but nevertheless influential places—as a responsibility to be avoided at all costs.

Until women were emancipated, they were generally trained only for the work they expected to do as
wives and mothers. A girl grew up in a household in
which she was taught the domestic arts—to cook and
sew, to wash clothing, and to care for children at home.
By the time she reached adulthood, she was trained to
be a homemaker in her own right. But she knew little
about the outside world. She could not run a typewriter
or adding machine or operate a telephone switchboard.
She knew nothing about the art of selling goods to customers in stores, and—needless to say—was not equipped
to pursue a career as a doctor or lawyer or even to work
on the assembly line in a factory.

All that has changed. It has been said that today's
typical bride hardly knows how to prepare an ordinary
dinner—and that without canned or packaged food, many
an American family would hover on the brink of starva-
tion. Nor is the modern young woman equipped to maintain her home, cook, sew, and care for children.

Statistics tell the story graphically. In 1890, only one
woman in six, aged twenty to sixty-four, was employed
outside the home. But by 1960, the number had jumped
to one in three.

Even more significant has been the steady rise in the
number of married women who work outside the home.
In 1900, only 15 per cent of the employed women were
married. Today, the number of married women exceeds
50 per cent. Moreover, more than one-third of all the
working women in the United States are mothers.

In the modern world, it is the "career woman"—not the mother and homemaker—who is the glamorous person. It is she who receives the publicity and whose work is made to seem creative and worth-while. The "career woman," we are told, does work which challenges her intellect, which is stimulating and not monotonous, and which enables her to perform a service for society.

It is true that many women make full use of their talents—for example, as doctors, nurses, teachers, librarians, social workers—and that many do work of great benefit to society in which they utilize the training received in college. But many of the jobs which women perform in offices and factories are less demanding intellectually and more deadening than maintaining a home. Quite often, a woman sits behind a typewriter all day to avoid the "drudgery" of teaching her own children—and is led to believe that it is glamorous. She may take a job on the assembly line, repeating the same task from the moment she enters the factory until she leaves it, to avoid the "monotony" of housework. She may stand on her feet all day behind a sales counter, striving to maintain her disposition with ill-tempered customers, because she can't stand her "demanding" children.

Regardless of these conditions, it is a fact that the average young woman of today fully expects to work outside the home until she marries, expects to work after marriage until she becomes pregnant, and may or may not plan to return to her job after her baby is born. She is quite likely to expect to return to work after the children have entered school and are gone from the house for six hours or so each day.

This preparation for and interest in gainful employment

means that the modern woman often must make a deliberate choice between a job outside the home and the having of babies which would necessitate her staying within it. The lure of the career often impels her to defer having children until she can spare the time, or to postpone childbirth indefinitely. Moreover, her income frequently leads to raising of the standards of living which she and her husband come to depend upon. Once they have become accustomed to living on two incomes, they may find it extremely difficult to face the prospect of living on one—and with another mouth to feed as well. The result? More pressure for the limitation of births.

Of course, no institution has been more active than the Church in fighting to uphold the dignity of women. Only in Christian societies—and as a result of Christian teaching—have women achieved equality with men. In other societies women are in an inferior position and sometimes are little better than chattels who can virtually be bought and sold at will.

The Church has always stressed the obligation of men to treat women with the dignity and justice that their human position entitles them to. Insofar as women's new freedom of women has eliminated evils which existed when men exercised complete control and denied their wives their just rights, the Church has completely approved. She does not object to the position of equality which women hold, but deplores the fact that as a by-product the emphasis has shifted from the basic vocation of wives—which is motherhood—and has encouraged them to follow a different path.

The world-wide trend toward secularization. This is the most insidious pressure of all, for it denies God, His existence, and His teaching. True, past generations did not always act in accord with His laws and permitted many offenses which cannot be condoned. But they never made it a basic article of belief that God did not exist, nor did they ever deny that He had any power to bind men on earth. This was true even in non-Christian cultures.

Today, however, in much of the area which is commonly but perhaps mistakenly called the Christian world, God is openly rejected. His teachings are ignored or scoffed at, and it is widely maintained that He can say nothing to us about the most important activities of our lives.

To prove the truth of this statement, one need look no farther than to divorce statistics. Until the beginning of this century, the divorce of a man and woman occurred rarely. When it did take place, it met with the general disapproval of society.

In other days, man and woman married with the understanding that they were entering upon a relationship for life. With this in mind, they were generally determined to adjust to their new state as best they could. They were prepared to make whatever sacrifices might be necessary to achieve a reasonable success of their marriage.

In this atmosphere, husbands and wives had no difficulty in accepting childbirth, because they knew that they were married for life and would have to share in bringing up the children. They often accepted offspring because they knew of the time-honored role that children can play in bringing a couple together—in transforming a man and woman from basically selfish, self-seeking creatures into responsible, sacrificing persons united in a bond of common love.

This situation is no longer true in a large part of society. No one of marrying age today can fail to be aware of the fact that divorces are easy to procure, and under the flimsiest pretexts. For example, it is well known that in any given year in the United States there is a record of one divorce to every four marriages begun. With this condition in mind, it is extremely difficult for the average young man and woman to enter marriage without at least a lingering thought that there is a way out of it. Whereas the nineteenth-century couple married with the idea of making it work, the twentieth-century couple marry with the idea of seeing if it will work—and of making other arrangement if it does not turn out as anticipated.

When marriages begin with this attitude of uncertainty, it is not hard to understand why many men and women are unwilling to have the child that would turn what is essentially their trial marriage into what could become a permanent arrangement, or at least one which would be more difficult to get out of—and, for the male, more costly as well. The ease with which divorces can be obtained, coupled with the ability of women to earn their own way in the working world, has tended to make wives less dependent upon their husbands. Insofar as a wife no longer need be a timid creature who must bow before every word from her lord and master, this is a good thing. But it has had the effect of making some women reason that they will lose their "equality" if they become pregnant. Moreover, they reason that if they take on the lifelong responsibilities of caring for a child, they may lose their freedom to discard its father in the future.

Catholics, of course, do not believe in divorce, because Christ taught "what therefore God has joined together, let no man put asunder." (Matthew, 19:6.) The Catholic who receives the sacrament of matrimony does so with the determination to make it a lifetime relationship. Nevertheless, he may seek a separation for valid reasons, and may also seek an annulment of the marriage if it was not valid in the first place. Each year, some 2000 Catholics seek an annulment from the matrimonial court of the New York archdiocese alone. Only a tiny percentage of these applications is granted, but their number suggests that the idea of getting out of a marriage which does not live up to expectations has affected Catholics as well.

The growing secularism is nowhere more evident than in the widespread belief that God made the marital act primarily for recreation. Such an emphasis on sex for its own sake is manifested in many ways: The determination of men and women to wring every ounce of pleasure out of the act, as evidenced by the widespread interest in techniques and positions, the experimenting with sensations; the widespread dissatisfaction, reported by doctors, of wives who fail to achieve a complete sensation every time they copulate, despite the fact that such an achievement never has been a realistic accomplishment; and by the growing incidence of infidelity resulting when one or both of the partners does not get as much pleasure from the marriage bed as expected.

Of course, a married couple should consciously strive to make their sexual union a satisfactory physical and emotional experience, for by doing so they strengthen their love for each other and thus further one of the purposes for which they married. The important consideration, from a Christian point of view, is that the spiritual and emotional union achieved by the act is of greater value than any purely physical sensations. It is a fact that if the spiritual and emotional adjustment of the partners is satisfactory, they will make a reasonably satisfactory physical adjustment. But if they emphasize the physical aspects, while minimizing its importance as a means of expressing the full depth of their love, they debase it by putting it on a purely animalistic level. As is seen so often when couples marry for physical reasons and without any strong spiritual and emotional bond, a union made for the enjoyment of sex is usually broken when the novelty wears off.

Moreover, when the physical enjoyment of sex is the only objective of intercourse, pregnancy becomes a catastrophe that must be avoided at all costs. Pregnancy frequently requires long periods of abstinence. A couple may be advised to abstain during the early stages of pregnancy if the doctor thinks there is a danger of miscarriage. They may be told to limit their relations during the middle months, and they will be obliged to abstain during the last six weeks of pregnancy and probably for three or four weeks after birth. In view of these factors, pregnancy becomes a thing to be avoided for those who believe that sex was made solely for pleasure.

The idea that sex is a game that everyone can—and even should—play has gained such wide support that marriage itself is more popular than ever. For example, in the United States, of every ten men twenty-five years old or older, only one has never been married, and only one woman in eleven of that age has never been married. To be sure, of those who have married, many are now divorced, separated, or widowed. But the fact that all but a very few are willing to take the plunge exemplifies the prevailing belief that a person without a sexual outlet is doomed somehow to frustration and neuroses of various kinds.

All available statistics on marriage and divorce are reliable indications that the Sacrament of Marriage is not seriously regarded by many people. In fact, the age at which people marry and the ease with which they enter and leave marriage, both suggest that they think that this union was made to enjoy, and can be discarded whenever enjoyment ceases. The added fact that millions of people are marrying each year with little or no adequate preparation indicates that they are not greatly interested in having children, and of leading a true Christian family life.

We can conclude from these facts that our dominant culture is moving towards a new definition of marriage and the family—one diametrically opposed to the concept which Christians have traditionally held. For many Americans, marriage has become a social arrangement. They argue that it has no divine origin and need obey no divine rules; that each marriage is a personal arrangement between two people who are free to do as they please; that it is an "instrument of personal fulfillment" and if the husband or wife decides that he or she no longer is being "fulfilled," he or she is perfectly free to terminate the arrangement. In their view, a thing like pregnancy should not interfere with their enjoyment of each other.

In view of the pressures we have cited—the industrialization of society; the changed status of women; and the secularization of our culture—the couple who strive to raise a family in the Christian tradition may feel that they are in the wrong time and place. In many cases, it requires genuine heroism to go against the crowd.

Forty years ago, when the culture was more friendly to our family ideals, individual Catholics were protected from some of these evil influences by the solidarity of their own environments. People followed their national and religious customs. They were married by the priest, had their children, and stayed married. The religious tenets of their faith were reflected in the social practices of the community. In doubt, they accepted the leadership of their priests without question.

Today there is no religious solidarity among Catholics. Each couple faces the hostile culture alone. Whereas before they followed the Catholic crowd, now they must make individual choices, oftentimes in the face of strong social pressures. Now they must approach personal decisions inside the family circle with greater understanding of their faith, higher motivation, and as much encouragement from the Catholic community as it is possible to give. Modern couples need a greater intellectuality, deeper spirituality, and more solidarity than their forebears. Otherwise they will be caught up in a whirlpool of destruction.

Catholics should understand these influences of modern life thoroughly. When they realize the factors at work in our civilization, they will be able more intelligently to appraise their own ability to fulfill their responsibilities of parenthood, to decide for themselves how many children they should have, and whether the time is now right for them to have a child.

4.

The World's Answer
—Contraception

DAVID AND JEAN began going steady when they sat
opposite each other as freshmen in high school. David
was then fourteen years old, and actually not much interested in girls. But the school had a program of activities which boys and girls were expected to attend together. Dave discovered that without a date he was "out
of it." So when Jean asked him to attend a dance with
her, he decided to go, particularly since he found that
she could help him with his homework.

Prodded a little by her mother, Jean soon turned "going steady" into a routine. Holding hands in time became
necking and petting. Inevitably there was intercourse.
Both felt a tug of conscience, but they convinced themselves that "they loved each other" and that "everybody
does it." Immediately after graduation they were married.

Now began some problems they did not anticipate.
They wanted an attractive home furnished as nicely as
their own parents' homes. They expected to have a car

and all of the modern labor-saving household appliances. Jean continued working, and to avoid having their plans upset, contraception entered their lives.

However, a child was conceived about a year after marriage and when Jean stayed home to care for the new baby, the family found itself on the brink of economic disaster. Dependent for so long on two salaries, they found it almost impossible to get by on one. Grandma then took over the baby and Jean returned to work. Now contraception became the most important thing in her life.

But life plays its tricks. In an unguarded moment, David and Jean conceived another baby. This shocked them. Jean had heard certain old wives' remedies for an unwanted baby. But the fetus would not be dislodged. A little conscience-stricken but determined nonetheless, she visited an abortionist who decided that she was too far gone to take any chances.

So David, Jr., was born. But Jean resolved never to be "caught" again. She made it her business to be sterilized before she came home from the hospital and within six months she was back to work and the children were back with her mother. Twelve years later the family moved to the suburbs and, while Jean sometimes wishes she could have another baby, this foursome has come to be known among their neighbors as an ideal family.

The story above, in all its detail, does not necessarily find its verification everywhere. But it is a composite of the viewpoints and experiences of thousands of American couples. And while relatively few couples might be so consistently callous, some part of this tale fits more actual domestic situations than we like to admit.

Statistics show that half of today's brides are twenty years of age or younger, and that the last child is born to the average American woman before she is twenty-eight. Most working women are married, and 40 per cent of the working wives come from families whose annual income is $10,000 or more. Two children, certainly no more than three, seem to represent the modern ideal. Family-planning usually means contraception or sterilization. And if they did not have married women to keep them prosperous, abortionists would lose 90 per cent of their business.

Contraception in one form or another, therefore, is the world's solution for all real and imagined family problems.

"THE TRAGEDY OF PREGNANCY"

It is unquestionably true that many people, particularly non-Catholics, use contraception (including sterilization and abortion) in good faith. They face real problems, have an easy answer at their finger tips, and find it difficult to see why they should not use the easy way. These are the hardship situations which are usually put forward as justifying causes for contraception. The public press is filled with tales of them, and the persons involved fill the offices of clergymen, doctors, and marriage counselors. Beset by heart-rending human difficulties and living in a culture that prizes efficiency more than righteousness, people tend to follow the line of least resistance. To them, the religious argument seems far removed from reality. To such people we can offer understanding and sympathy, and when they are ready for it, a little better advice.

But let us be truthful, too. Such "hardship cases" are far from the majority, although all couples using artificial means of birth prevention like to identify themselves with hardship. It is more correct to say that in the world's view, a baby is often the worst thing that can happen to a couple—certainly a third, fourth, or fifth baby is a calamity. Many sophisticated plays and novels make the discovery of pregnancy a turning point in the relationship of a husband and wife, changing what was pleasurable and happy into a nightmare of drudgery and self-sacrifice. As a result of such thinking, for every couple with legitimate reasons for not having children, there are many more who do not want babies or more babies for materialistic reasons.

To the devoted Christian couple, the story of David and Jean may read like fantasy. It is difficult for one who accepts the supremacy of God to believe that people would marry with such little consideration of its sacred character. Yet each year millions of young people enter what they believe to be a lifelong relationship with not much greater concern than they show in buying a house, and sometimes with even less concern. A couple should never regard childbearing with horror. Yet, estimates that there are nearly a million abortions annually in the United States indicate that many wives are willing to commit murder to prevent a birth. For those who believe that a mother's guidance is the greatest influence a child may ever have, it is difficult to understand why so many babies are turned over to others, even complete strangers, while the mother works and makes sure at the same time that her way of life will not be interrupted by pregnancies again.

Yet many otherwise nice people hold these secular points of view—people who are well mannered, well dressed, well educated, in fact the "best people" in town. Basic to their approval of contraception, divorce, and allied evils, is the assumption then an unwanted pregnancy is a fate almost worse than death.

How can we explain this? We can only deplore the fact that the modern worldly establishment rejects the primacy of God, conscience, and religion. As one man of dubious beliefs put it: "I believe in God, but I can't accept his telling me how to care for myself on earth."

THE POINT OF DEPARTURE

Here we come to the nub of the problem:

Apart from God, His law, and our religious traditions, plus our ultimate responsibility to Him for our actions, no case can be made against contraception, or for that matter, against murder, homosexuality or any moral evil. For without God, morals are only what society says they are, and then only for the moment.

Let the record show that the whole contraceptive movement began with agnostics and socialists, whose hatred of religion and family life are well known. It should also be realized that many vocal evangelists of contraception today are not known for their religious piety. In fact, they represent modern agnosticism and socialism, although the latter has often been replaced by the softer word "liberal," much the same as "planned parenthood" is today considered more acceptable than "contraception." But let us not be deluded into separating contraception from sterilization or abortion and, in time, from the elimination of the sick and the aged (nicely called "euthanasia"), for one follows the other as the night follows day. And if we note that some religious leaders have "baptized" a movement that originated in irreligion, it is not without noting also that God constantly has had to send prophets and reformers to scourge those who worship strange gods.

WHAT IS GOD'S PLAN FOR MAN?

The true Christian believes that God had a purpose in creating man and woman. Made in His image and likeness and after a life on earth, they are destined to enjoy His Beatitude throughout eternity.

He created two sexes. But this does not mean that He sent them off to work out their purposes without any reference to Him. Marital intercourse became God's way of creating successors to Adam and Eve—and if His Command "increase and multiply" means anything, He expected man and woman to be generous with this gift.

There is no other way for babies to be born except through the union of male and female. (Only the same omnipotent atheist believes that the test tube, invented out of man's God-given genius, is a proper substitute for the basic human relationship of marriage.) Examine that marital union rationally and objectively. It is ordained to the conception of human life. Man and woman may or may not copulate, but when they do they merge with the basic forces of nature. They become wrapped up in the mystery of life. They take on a power greater than either has singly. They put themselves in God's hands. Their rapture goes beyond the ecstasy of the moment because, if God wills it and His new image is created by His direct intervention with a human soul, even the angels sing.

Certainly they love each other. Otherwise they would not be there. Each union symbolizes that love, indeed strengthens it. The physical relaxation is important, but NOT so important as the spiritual refreshment, the renewal of kindly feeling, the blotted memory of past offenses, the general sense of well-being that redounds even to the advantage of the other children.

But—and this is a big "but"—they may not love each other while they hate God. They may not take God to the bedroom door and slam the door in His face. What was given by God out of His goodness and to magnify the generosity of their personality, may not become an instrument of calculated selfishness, the only purpose allowed being personal gratification or convenience. To use a precious gift with injury to the Divine Donor is ingratitude of the rankest kind.

Moreover, the contraceptive does not unite. It divides. It involves taking, not giving. It makes the marital act the union of sexual organs, not the merging of devoted human personalities. The marriage bed becomes not a sanctuary in which two lovers consecrate themselves anew to the Heavenly Father Who made all this possible, but a chamber of lust. And practitioners of contraception, regardless of what they say in public, sense that their union is somehow unclean.

A man eats to satisfy his hunger. He eats not for the

sake of eating, but to live, even when he does not think of this or when his food is not actually nourishing. So man and wife ordain themselves by intercourse to parenthood, even when they are not thinking of a child, or when the conception of a child is in fact impossible.

If God had intended the sexual experience for pleasure, without any regard for the propagation of mankind, He would have made it so that it could be enjoyed for its own sake alone. There are such pleasures in life. Music need serve no other purpose but the pleasure it gives to the composer, player, or hearer. Natural beauty often serves little other purpose than to delight the beholder. Had God wished sex to be used primarily for pleasure, He would have devised different means of creating men.

But He did not do this. He tied conception to marital intercourse. Men were free to marry or not. Married men were free to copulate or not. But copulation of its nature, regardless of its pleasurable aspects, was pointed to the mysterious work of creation. God's basic and first command to Adam and Eve: "Increase and multiply, and fill the earth" makes that very clear. The basic evil of contraception is that it makes God's purposes subordinate to those of men—it has man using sex in a way which may suit man's pleasure-seeking purposes but which defeats the purposes God had in mind.

This being so, artificial barriers against the natural completion of the marriage act are contrary to God's will because the people using them put second things first. The sin involved is not so much that God's will is not done (it is not always easy to know what His will is) but that God is prevented from having any power over creation at all. The sexual faculty, endowed by Him with an objective function, is used in such a way as to exclude positively and completely its natural fulfillment. Pope Pius XI developed the argument in this way: "Since the conjugal act is destined primarily by nature for the begetting of children, those who in exercising it deliberately frustrate its natural power and purpose, sin against nature, and commit a deed which is shameful and intrinsically evil."

Whatever practical advantage accrues to the users (and sin of every kind always brings some momentary reward) experience shows that contraceptive intercourse is a threat to the sacred nature of marriage itself, even to the sexual morals of the unmarried. The contraceptionist says in effect: "My personal, physical, or emotional well-being comes first. Little else counts for much." And this without any real discipline on his part. "Why not use modern science to keep away an unwanted pregnancy?" he argues. But note the emphasis is on indulgence, not control. He no longer looks upon himself as a spiritual being with the power within himself to be lord of his passions, as he was intended to be master of everything under heaven. And he makes God an outsider to the whole process.

What does contraception imply for the husband? It implies that he must be satisfied when and as he pleases. It implies that man is basically an animal incapable of real love which sometimes involves sacrifice of convenience.

And what does it imply for the wife? While pretending to liberate her from the excessive burdens of marriage (this was Margaret Sanger's great complaint), contraception makes her as never before a real sex object for man,

not his helpmate and mother of his children. And if
women of old rarely could control thoughtless husbands,
the new woman has given up the fight for equality in the
sex relationship. She is now content to submit, as long as
she is not mother. This is the real offense to womanly dignity implicit in all forms of contraception.

And so we make artificial birth control an evil deed by
its very nature. Like murder, blasphemy, adultery, no excuse can justify it or permit its use. And when practiced,
the offense against God is a mortal sin, because it involves
a serious disorder in the marital relationship.

Here we deal not with Church law, but with God's
moral law. A thousand years from now we may be eating
meat on Friday and Catholic priests may be married men,
because these practices flow out of the man-made law of
the Church, enacted for particular disciplinary reasons.
But in the year 3000, murder, blasphemy, adultery—and
contraception—will still be mortal sins because even then
God's law will stand firm, awaiting our obedience.

WHY MAN MUST OBEY "NATURAL LAW"

God runs His universe through law. It is the only
way things can be run properly. He has two groups of
laws which need concern us here—*the laws of nature* for
things and the *moral laws* for man.

We all take the laws of nature for granted. If we
do not eat, we die. If we expose ourselves to extreme
cold, we freeze. If we jump from a tall building, we fall.
And so on.

God also wants men to live in certain ways. He gave

us the gift of reason, the prophets of old and the Church to help us know those ways. The moral laws of God (found basically in the Ten Commandments) apply to *all* human beings, just as all men are bound by the laws of gravity.

This point is vital *because many persons* think that contraception is a sin only for Catholics. *Contraception is a sin for everyone.* When the Church points to all men that this particular law exists, she is like the men who warns another about jumping from a building. The man merely calls attention to the law of gravity which will exist to the end of time even if no one called attention to it.

Many people, even Catholics, mistakenly believe that sometime the Church will change her mind on this matter. This is wishful thinking. The law of God on contraception as expressed through human reason and His official spokesman will stand today and forever.

CONTRACEPTION HAS ALWAYS BEEN CONSIDERED EVIL

The belief that artificial birth control violates Divine Law has existed from Old Testament times until the present day. It will surprise many to discover that men decided otherwise *only very recently.*

The ancient Hebrews considered fruitfulness to be the greatest of God's gifts and any form of contraception was unthinkable. The Old Testament abounds in blessings like that which the Creator gave to Adam and Eve. Three times God gave Noah His blessing, "Be fruitful and multiply." (Genesis 8:17; 9:1; 9:7.) In His first words to Abraham, God promised: "I will make of thee a great nation." (Genesis, 12:2.) God also told Abraham, "I will make thy seed as the dust of the earth." (Genesis, 13:16) and "Look up to heaven and number the stars, if thou canst. So shall thy seed be!" (Genesis, 15:5.) After Abraham offered to sacrifice his son Isaac if need be, God promised him anew: "I will bless thee, and I will multiply thy seed as the stars of heaven, and as the sand that is by the seashore." (Genesis, 22:17.) The blessings of children were promised to Isaac and Jacob and to Ishmael and Rebecca. The belief that the woman with many children is among the most fortunate of creatures is illustrated by the blessing her own family gave to Rebecca: "Mayest thou increase to thousands of thousands." (Genesis, 24:60.)

Inasmuch as parenthood was considered so enormous a privilege, contraception was regarded as one of the worst sins a Hebrew could commit. Contraception today is often called "onanism," from the Biblical story of Onan, son of Judah, who spilled his seed on the ground, rather than have complete intercourse with his dead brother's wife, and was killed by God for his sin.

From the days of the Apostles, there was never any doubt among Christians that the use of contraceptive methods was a mortal sin. In the fifth century, St. Augustine flatly stated: "Intercourse, even with one's legitimate wife, is unlawful and wicked when the conception of offspring is prevented." The Angelic Doctor of the Church, St. Thomas Aquinas, one of the great minds of all times, argued that deliberate contraception, next to abortion, was the greatest vice in marriage. In 1566, the Council of Trent warned explicitly against "the most serious sin committed by those who prevent conception."

Until very recently all Christians and Jews were of one mind regarding contraception. Even Thomas Robert Malthus, the Anglican clergyman who, in 1798, first warned about a possible population explosion, opposed contraception as a means of controlling population growth. He wrote that intercourse in which an effort is made to prevent birth "seems to lower in the most marked manner the dignity of human nature."

In our own time, Pope Pius XI stated, in 1930, that "any use whatsoever of matrimony exercised in such a way that the act is deliberately frustrated in its natural power to generate life is an offense against the law of God and of nature, and those who indulge in such are branded with the guilt of grave sin."

LIBERAL CHRISTIANITY AND REFORM JEWRY

Until the present century, no important religious leader would have seriously argued that contraception was a moral method of family limitation. All churches were united against it, and for the reasons that the Catholic Church is against it today.

In fact, when Margaret Sanger began, in 1912, to make "birth control" the work of her lifetime, few persons who valued their reputations would have anything to do with her movement. A large percentage of the early contraceptionists were atheists and violent anti-Christians, Socialists, anarchists, and proponents of the freest kind of free love. So close were the early ties of this movement with the forces of irreligion that it remains difficult today to appreciate the respectability of "planned parenthood" among non-Catholic religious groups.

For example, among Mrs. Sanger's early associates could be found such as Havelock Ellis, who believed that free sex experiment should precede every marriage. In an article called "Sex Problems of Modern Parents," he even advocated that parents show their children how to use contraceptives. Another pioneer contraceptionist was Bertrand Russell, who favored the idea that no marriage should be considered legal unless a couple could produce a medical certificate proving that the woman was pregnant! Still another was Dr. Samuel D. Schmalhausen, a leading figure in the World League for Sexual Reform, who declared that "it is no longer permissible for an enlightened person to be horrified by perversion."

Some of Mrs. Sanger's own social philosophy as she began her crusade may be deduced from her statement that "the whole structure of present-day society is built upon a rotten and decaying foundation. Until the evils of capitalism are swept away, there is no hope for young working girls to live a beautiful life."

The acceptance of Mrs. Sanger's cause by non-Catholic religious groups is not merely a permissible adjustment to family-planning as such (culture always plays a role in determining family size), but a radical reappraisal of the theology on contraception and marriage. And here the conscientious historian faces real difficulty in explaining these new departures.

Typical of the change that has come over non-Catholic groups are the decisions reached over the years by the Lambeth Conferences of the Church of England. It was only in 1908 that this authoritative Anglican body issued an encyclical which viewed contraception "with repugnance" and assailed it as "an evil which places home life in jeopardy." It condemned without reservation all forms of artificial birth control and stated that "deliberate tampering with nascent life is repugnant to Christian morality." In 1914, contraception again was condemned as "dangerous, demoralizing and sinful."

In 1920, another Lambeth Conference expressed alarm at the growth of contraceptive "theories and practices hostile to the family." It pointed out that procreation was the primary purpose of marriage.

Just ten years later, however, another conference of the Anglican leaders stated that "we cannot condemn the use of scientific methods for preventing conception which are thoughtfully and conscientiously adopted" if there is "a good moral reason" why the "way of abstinence should not be followed."

The wall had been breached. Once it was concluded that there might be moral justification for contraception in exceptional cases, the exceptions grew more and more numerous. So much so, in fact, that in 1958 it conceded that the use of contraceptives in family-planning could be "admissible to the Christian conscience." What was a grievous sin little more than fifty years ago now is not only not a sin, but may even be a "moral duty." And in the country where this Church exerts its greatest influence, all kinds of contraceptive devices are now displayed and advertised in shop windows.

A similar retreat from the moral principles held from the beginning of time until this present century has been made by many Jews. But we would be mistaken if we assumed that all but Catholics have changed to the "new morality." Many conservative Protestants and Jews as well as members of the Orthodox Greek religion maintain that artificial contraception is inherently evil. For example, the Protestant writer, Dr. John R. Rice, wrote in his book, *The Home:*

"It is true that some leaders in the Federal Council of Churches in America have advocated birth control. But these leaders did not really represent Christianity nor the Christian feeling and conviction of the true Churches of Christ in America. They were modernists, denying every fundamental of the Christian Faith."

As regards the growth of the "contraceptive cult," the Orthodox Hebrew Rabbi Herbert S. Goldstein stated:

"Birth control is a violation of fundamental principles of traditional Orthodox Judaism. The economic reasons and over-population cited by advocates of birth control are satanic."

THE BASIS OF THE NEW THEOLOGY

Several reasons, rooted in Protestant philosopy and practice, may explain why the contraceptionists were able to make rapid headway within half a century—moving from disreputable beginnings to popular acceptance by leading non-Catholic philosophies. One factor, obviously, is the basic Protestant tenet that faith in God alone is sufficient for salvation. Once a man accepts Christ as his Savior, it is argued, personal conduct can do little to help him achieve salvation or to lose it. In fact, John Cal-

vin based his whole theory of predestination on the belief
that God had already determined the eternal destiny of
all of us, regardless of personal merit. In such circumstances, good deeds become "nice" rather than the necessarily right thing to do and resistance to evil tends to
crumble under sustained pressure.

Furthermore, in the face of the practical difficulties
faced by many women during pregnancy, Protestant
theologians began to reason that the coequal if not the
primary purpose of matrimony is the happiness of the
couple—not the procreation and education of children.
From such a promise, it is easy to make artificial marital
intercourse unrelated to conception a matter of primary
importance, and parenthood subordinate to the well-being
of the couple. This argument also explains the Protestant
penchant for divorce.

And since the contraceptive movement proved to be
popular, the church which made much of its "democ-
racy" found itself following people, rather than leading
them. Most of us forget that God did not act democrati-
cally when He created us. Without consulting men, He
established the rules by which we must live. And in His
Ten Commandments, He made no provision for us to
change His rules whenever it became inconvenient to
abide by them.

It is no coincidence that the widespread acceptance
of contraception had occurred simultaneously with what
had come to be known as "The Age of Easy Living."
Some social scientists have made a fetish of comfort, and
they consider sacrifice and moral restraint as unacceptable
with modern needs. A young man seeking his first job
is likely to talk to his prospective employer about vacations

and other benefits—even retirement plans—with some obvious distaste for hard work.

Contraception fits perfectly into this age which exalts pleasure over responsibility and prefers the enjoyable to the virtuous. In the minds of many advocates of birth control, it is folly for a young couple to marry with a willingness to make sacrifices at the expense of pleasure—to practice self-control in marriage when it is more enjoyable to let sex run on and on. How, therefore, can we expect a world which rejects the supernatural viewpoint on parenthood to think highly of the positive work of having babies?

As to the Jewish position, more and more Orthodox believers are distressed at the inroads made on Reform Jewry by secular influences. We have only to remember how the Apostles came to Christ with their query about the Mosaic permission for divorce. Far from acceding to the argument that indissoluble marriage is too difficult, Christ replied: "Moses, by reason of the hardness of your heart, permitted you to put away your wives; but it was not so from the beginning." (Matthew, 19:8.) Christ redeclared the basic moral law and made it His law. He would make the same response to modern Jews using that kind of argument to relax the moral law.

CONTRACEPTION AND THE STATE

The highly financed, well-organized efforts of "Planned Parenthood" groups to get governmental bodies to promote contraception on a world-wide scale may surprise some. But strong tinges of such social planning have been found in the Sanger movement from the beginning. Many people like to run others' lives, telling them how they should act in their most intimate relationships. And when one realizes the early close connection between socialist groups and the Sanger organization, the connection seems almost natural. There are many supporters of the movement today who see contraception as a means by which the state can take over the procreative process, telling couples how many children to have and when to have them. In this way, "undesirable" elements can be kept from having too many children.

Mrs. Sanger toyed with the idea herself. She wrote an article in the *American Weekly* of May 27th, 1934, in which she proposed an "American baby code" which contained the following articles:

"*Article 3.* A marriage shall in itself give husband and wife only the right to a common household and not the right to parenthood.

"*Article 4.* No woman shall have the legal right to bear a child and no man shall have the right to become a father without a permit for parenthood.

"*Article 6.* No permit shall be valid for more than one birth."

These views tell much about the family philosophy of contraceptive leaders—a philosophy which flows out of concepts on sex and marriage completely alien to Western civilization.

ARTIFICIAL METHODS OF CONTRACEPTION

Because Catholics sometimes use artificial methods without realizing that they are forbidden, it is important to know precisely what a contraceptive method is.

A contraceptive method is one which interferes in some way with the natural act of intercourse. Normally the substance of the husband is deposited in the vagina of the wife. The contraceptive seeks to do one or more of four things: To impede ovulation or the development of fertile sperm; to prevent the deposit of semen into the vaginal orifice; to prevent the semen from traveling upward through the womb; or to destroy the semen after it has been deposited. In each case, the dominant and primary purpose of husband or wife is to prevent the possible union of sperm and ovum.

Efforts to thwart the natural law are almost as old as mankind. Dr. John R. Cavanaugh, prominent psychiatrist and author, states that some Egyptians thought that a woman could avoid conception if she applied a paste made from the dung of crocodiles or elephants. Among the Greeks, rubbing olive oil into the walls of the vagina was thought to destroy the seed. Ancient Turks applied to the cervix a sponge soaked with lemon juice. In Palestine, Hebrew prostitutes considered that postcoital gryrations could dislodge the semen. Even today, some persons believe that without female orgasm conception is unlikely, although, according to Dr. Carl G. Hartman, noted medical author, there is no scientific basis for this impression.

While crude "contraceptives" were known in early societies, their use was the exception rather than the rule. In many cases, they were developed and employed only by prostitutes. In fact, until recent times probably the greatest crime a wife could commit was to use a contraceptive. Some peoples regarded this matter so seriously that the wife who sought to avoid having a baby often received the death penalty.

It was not until the nineteenth century that the knowledge of mechanical contraceptive methods was given wide distribution in any social group. When Margaret Sanger went to Paris in 1913, her biographer says, she went searching for methods of contraception and collected formulas for douches and techniques in the use of suppositories and pessaries. These were virtually unknown in America at that time.

In the modern era, the commonly used and well-known methods of contraception are: By the man, deliberate withdrawal during intercourse or use of the condom (sheath); by the woman, insertion of the diaphragm, vaginal jellies, creams, tablets and suppositories of all kinds, tampons, and taking of a douche. Use of these contraceptives always involves mortal sin.

Recently much has been written about a progestational steroid, popularly known as "the pill" or by a trade name—Enovid, Norlutin, etc. This drug is synthetic material which acts like a natural hormone (progesterone). When taken by mouth for twenty days out of each monthly cycle, it keeps the woman from ovulating. Without ovulation, there can be no conception. Although the sexual act of people using this chemical is normal, its sustained use sterilizes the woman.

Drugs of this kind may serve other purposes. They help women to ovulate who otherwise would not do so or would do so rarely. In fact, the original research in this field grew out of a desire to help women become fertile. After a woman's ovarian functions were suppressed for several months, it was discovered that in many cases she was likely to ovulate more readily when she stopped taking the drug. Thus her chances of conception increased. Doctors have also discovered that this chemical inhibits excessive uterine bleeding, relieves excessive menstrual pain, and protects an already formed pregnancy.

In all cases like these where a real pathology exists, the use of this drug is not only medically indicated but morally quite proper. Unquestionably, temporary sterility results. *But this indirect effect is not intended.* It is merely permitted. Consequently, good medicine is also good morals, since the correction of physical defects or the cure of physical disease is always laudatory.

However, when it was discovered that this drug leads to sterility, it became highly popular among doctors and patients—not as a curative agent, but as a contraceptive. And there is little doubt that its primary use now in hospitals, doctors' offices, and private homes is to prevent conception.

Catholics must be apprised of the fact that the use of steroids merely to prevent conception is immoral, and no less reprehensible than the use of other artificial contraceptives. The reason is simple: No one has the right to mutilate his body or to change the function of an organ unless disease is present. Obviously, if the user's ovaries are healthy, she intends to sterilize herself when she uses "the pill." She should no more countenance steroids than the surgical removal of her ovaries or the hysterectomy of a healthy womb. The fact that one sterilization is temporary while the other is permanent does not change the morals of the act. She cannot deliberately have sterile intercourse by artificial means.

The principle of moral behavior in the case mentioned is fairly clear. Steroids can be used to cure pathology but not for contraception. But less scrupulous doctors or patients, by playing loose with the facts, find more ample justification for the use of these chemicals than concrete situations sometimes warrant. For example, doctors and patients, even Catholics, sometimes allege or enlarge on minor symptoms such as a slight uterine bleeding or menstrual pain so as to use these drugs more readily.

A common excuse for their use is that they help regularize monthly cycles and therefore enable conscientious women to practice the rhythm method more effectively. This is not quite true. The drug may regularize monthly bleeding, but no known drug can induce regular ovulation. Even if she menstruates every twenty-five to thirty days, a woman still must concern herself with irregular ovulation which produced the irregular bleeding in the first place. Consequently, allegations that progestational steroids enable people to determine ovulation more readily (which is basic to the effective practice of periodic continence) are false.

The purity of the doctor's intention (and of the patient's) is manifest in the length of time during which the dosage is prescribed. Manufacturers suggest three months, after which the pill must be withdrawn to see if expected medical effect has been realized. But if this pill is taken month after month or year after year without interruption, one may reasonably presume that the primary intent is not to correct some pathology but to prevent conception.

OTHER CONSIDERATIONS

Apart from the fact that the use of contraceptive devices is a serious sin, a certain amount of trouble and unpleasantness is connected with each of them. Perhaps these practical objections, plus their own "small silent voice" which tells them they are doing wrong, make many contraceptive-users more than a little annoyed.

Certainly there is nothing esthetic about a contraceptive. Even if it did not intrude on some phase of married love (and it always does), unnatural intercourse becomes an exercise with physical apparatus rather than a free, unimpeded giving of one person's self to the other. The condom of its nature implies interruption. Diaphragms or jellies require careful preparation, possibly many hours in advance. Withdrawal or douching destroy unity.

And what is worse, the whole process tends to emphasize the physical aspects of the act. The emotional union, the sense of mutual giving, is impaired when there must be concern about whether this or that device will function properly.

We hear much about the difficulties associated with periodic continence but little about the difficulties with contraceptives mentioned above or about the risk of failure involved in their use. Use of the rhythm method has its limits, but so have mechanical means of prevention. There is no such thing as the perfect contraceptive, as their advocates willingly admit. Imperfect products and loosely fitted devices—and carelessness in their use—all contribute to the births of so-called unwanted babies.

The progestational steroid pills are supposed to be the most effective method yet developed. Yet they will not work unless a woman follows instructions to the letter. If she stops taking them even for a few days, her chances of becoming pregnant are greatly increased. And there are undesirable side effects as well as unknown long-range dangers. While the pills have been in use only a short time, intestinal troubles, nausea, and feeling of bloatedness have been reported by some users. Moreover, doctors have every right to be concerned about long-range effects. The tragic side effects of thalidomide, the seemingly innocent sleeping pill which was responsible in 1962 for hundreds of deformed babies, are good grounds for caution in the use of any wonder drug.

As of this writing, 238 cases of thrombophlebitis or blood clotting among women taking Enovid have been reported by U.S. physicians. Twenty-four of these women died. Contraceptive-minded Norway has even banned the sale of Enovid. One doctor, after making a private poll of medical men in the Chicago area, found that a majority of them would not give these pills to their wives or daughters.

All of these signs indicate how cautious we all must be in prescribing or using new drugs, particularly when such use might be immoral as well as dangerous. Commercial firms are introducing new drugs every year sometimes with great financial profits to themselves, drugs which

later on are discontinued for medical reasons. Few, unfortunately, are discontinued for moral reasons.

Each succeeding year will bring a new host of medica-
tions designed to assist or inhibit ovulation or its determination. One of the latest is called Duphaston, designed
to regularize monthly bleeding *without* inhibiting ovulation. Should its claims prove to be correct, it would put
an end once and for all to the misuse of Enovid for purposes of regularization. Conscientious doctors would no
longer be justified in prescribing it for this purpose. At
all events, as patients sometimes get used to laxatives
and end up no better off at the end than they were in the
beginning, so we can expect that birth-control-minded
women, who think their salvation rests with a pill, may
find themselves ultimately weighted down by more serious problems, e.g., postponement of menopause for ten
to twenty years. The "ovulation-inducer" or the steroid will never be anything which can be taken like as-
pirin. Consequently, it might be well to remember that
by and large the cheapest, safest, most proper method of
fertility control is people control, and that human beings
cannot hope to solve their human problems by relying
more on drug addiction than on their own spiritual resources.

CONTRACEPTION AS A WAY OF LIFE

The introduction of contraception into our society has
resulted in radical changes in our thinking and our way
of life. In fact, whatever may be the earthly or temporal
advantages associated with contraception, profound evil

effects have followed in its wake. These evils deserve consideration not only by people considering their use but by social leaders who have ignored long-range results for immediate gain.

One of the major trends of our time has been the tendency to deny that the basic purpose of marriage is the procreation and education of children. Spokesmen carried along by a wave of secularism seem to make the enjoyment of intercourse an end in itself, even arguing that before God commanded Adam to "increase and multiply," He decided that it was "not good for man to be alone." According to this viewpoint, the well-being of the couple comes first, and marriage becomes more socially desirable than morally necessary. In the words of Bertrand Russell, "the use of contraceptives (makes) it increasingly possible to prevent sexual intercourse from leading to pregnancy and is therefore enabling women, if unmarried, to avoid children altogether, and if married to have children only by their husbands, without in either case finding it necessary to be chaste." The same author exulted that "contraceptives have altered the whole aspect of sex and marriage." When we read of publications like one called *Sex and the Single Girl*, we can sense the extent to which this notion is being pushed.

Propaganda idealizing contraception as a way of life has reached most American teen-agers. They know that devices exist to make intercourse somewhat safe. Formerly, potent forces kept unmarried people from premarital relations. When they were not moved by a positive appreciation for marriage, they were guided by the fear of offending God, the fear of pregnancy, or the fear of disease. Thanks to the secularists who have separated

science from morals, these preventive forces are weaker
than ever before. Young people hear that there is no such
thing as sin, that contraceptives are foolproof and sani-
tary, and that penicillin quickly conquers venereal dis-
eases contracted in sexual relations. While what they
hear is untrue, the result of such propaganda is an almost
incredible increase in immorality among the young—in
fact, appalling numbers of young people hold that sexual relations are proper for unmarried people "as long as
they love each other."

The "safety" of contraceptives is not borne out by the
cold fact that in the United States during a time when
social scientists were noting the growing use of contraceptives among unmarried American youth more than
200,000 illegitimate babies were born in 1958—more than
double the number for 1938. Further, a survey made in
1962 by Dr. George Gallup revealed that of married
women in their twenties, only one in four believes that an
absolutely sure method of birth control of any kind exists.
Their own experiences bear this out. Although most of the
women interviewed by Dr. Gallup and his researchers
approved some form of birth limitation, 56 per cent had
an "unplanned" first child—and 62 per cent reported that
other children in the family "just happened."

Nor is the highly publicized "quick cure" for venereal
disease evident in figures published by the New York De-
partment of Health showing that the number of cases of
venereal disease reported in 1961 represent a 431 per cent
increase over 1957!

If sex can be separated from marriage, it is also logical
to expect increased rates of marital infidelity and divorce
whenever one partner becomes bored with the other's sex-

ual performance and seeks more pleasurable contacts else-
where. All available sources of information indicate that
this is exactly what is happening. As Dr. Samuel D.
Schmalhausen of the World League for Sexual Reform
declared, "the complete divorce between sex and sin becomes the most significant moral phenomenon of modern
life."

It is not surprising that in two contraceptive cultures—
pagan Rome's and our own—we notice a high incidence
of homosexuality. The idea that sex organs are made for
pleasure and not procreation makes homosexual as well
as heterosexual activity quite natural. And this is what
homophiles (as they call themselves) maintain. They
have even established organizations to promote acceptance of their viewpoint. The author Jess Stearn wrote his
book, *The Sixth Man,* out of research that led him to
conclude that out of every six American males today one
is a homosexual.

It is commonly held that homosexuality is due to the
absence of a strong father figure in the child's experience,
and in individual cases this may well be so. But all centuries and peoples have had their weak fathers. For
example, Italy and Spain most likely have a fair share without having the amount of homosexuality found in Sweden, England, or the United States. The founder of psy-
chiatry, Sigmund Freud himself, warned that sex was not
an innocent game that anyone can play. In his *General
Introduction to Psychoanalysis,* he gave this more profound explanation of our present plight: "The common
characteristic of all perversions is that they have abandoned reproduction as their aim. We term sexual activity
perverse when it has renounced the aim of reproduction

and follows the pursuit of pleasure as an independent goal."

It is no coincidence that 70 per cent of all divorces granted are given to childless couples. Sexual union, created by God to serve parenthood and the eternal values, becomes an instrument of selfishness, and so does the marriage rooted in this poisonous soil. Can we be surprised, therefore, when a long life together becomes a frightening specter and sex a terrible bore? Not having a particular baby does not kill a marriage. In fact, a virtuous couple facing the difficult decision to avoid parenthood for a time can grow even closer together by their common need to be prudent, disciplined, and co-operative. But contraceptive intercourse involves no sacrifice and no real co-operation, because basically it is a divisive element in married love.

We now live in the age of the two-child family and the emancipated woman. The family of five is considered an unnatural monstrosity and their mother something of a freak. But those who come from an earlier generation and compare family with family and mother with mother are not sure that the advantages lie with the new products. No one can seriously doubt that small families are better for some people. But taking the grand view, we cherish life in the large family we remember nostalgically and which, if contraception continues on its way, will soon be a mere footnote in the history books.

THE NEXT STEP:
ABORTION AND STERILIZATION

More and more, abortion and sterilization form one way of life with contraception. The connection between all three is quite intimate. The same people who promote the one, defend the other. And the person who is aborted or sterilized almost always is someone previously committed to a contraceptive marriage. Dr. Alfred Kinsey, Dr. Raymond S. Pearl, and the Millbank Research Studies supply abundant evidence of the relationship.

The relationship between these three forms of birth prevention was not always so intimate. High-minded people, while allowing themselves to be persuaded to abandon the traditional Christian view on contraception, have always had a horror of abortion and sterilization. In fact, the Sangerite movement began with solemn promises that if women could be allowed the use of contraceptives, they would have no need for abortions.

Passing time, however, has shown that once basic religious principles are denied, it is just as easy to rationalize away the murder of an unborn infant as it is to argue against his conception. For a time, evangelists of such new morality may suffer some embarrassment (as the early birth-controllers did) but with success comes the righteous assurance that abortion is not only permissible but a high moral duty. This judgment may seem farfetched. But Japan, which was revamped by American social planners after World War II and given large doses of contraceptive medicine, in 1955 bore 1,727,040 new citizens while legally terminating the unborn lives of 1,170,143 others!

The recent attention given by "Planned Parenthood" spokesmen to the "population explosion" seems designed to soften the public's attitude toward sterilization, as it was softened toward contraceptives. In this regard, Richard M. Fagley, a Congregational minister and author of *The Population Explosion and Christian Responsibility*, commented: "As the population pressures mount, interest in, and support for, this solution continue to grow. Some states in India are offering bounties to parents agreeing to sterilization after the third or fourth child. Unless a technical 'breakthrough' is achieved in regard to a really suitable and acceptable contraceptive, an increase of pressure for sterilization seems to me virtually certain."

Because of the moral and social evils associated with these practices, they deserve special treatment.

The deliberate killing of an unborn child, any time after it has been conceived and prior to its birth, is abortion. Miscarriages are sometimes called *spontaneous* abortions, but such unplanned accidents of nature do not concern us here. Nor are we concerned with the surgical operation known as hysterectomy, in which the life of a fetus is indirectly terminated. This is not the intention of the operation, hence is not sinful abortion. What does concern us is when an unborn child is willfully and directly destroyed. All those responsible for such a murder, if they are Catholic, and this includes husband, midwife, and nurse, as well as doctor and patient, commit a *reserved sin*—that is, one reserved to the bishop for its forgiveness.

The extent of the practice of sinful abortion is appalling. Because the taking of an innocent life is illegal in many countries, precise figures of the abortions performed each year are impossible to obtain. Frederick J. Taussig, noted student of the question, gives us the number 700,000 in the United States alone—and this is certainly a conservative calculation. But it indicates for every five American babies born in any given year, one other has been intentionally killed during its mother's pregnancy.

In addition to these criminal acts, many abortions are termed "therapeutic." They are performed in secular hospitals by licensed physicians who believe that in allowing the pregnancy to reach its natural conclusion there would be increased danger to the life of the mother. About 18,000 therapeutic abortions are done in the United States each year.

Here is an area in which there is no agreement among doctors. Dr. S. A. Cosgrove, formerly head of obstetrics at Columbia University and past medical director of the Margaret Hague Maternity Hospital in Jersey City, and a non-Catholic, jolted the medical profession many years ago by condemning the tendency of American doctors to resort to abortion whenever they faced complicated pregnancies. In his hospital only eight therapeutic abortions were reported in 100,000 births. He abandoned such operations there in 1939. So impressive were the accomplishments of Hague Hospital that Dr. R. J. Heffernan of Tufts College said to the Congress of the American College of Surgeons in 1951: "Anyone who performs a therapeutic abortion is either ignorant of modern methods of treating the complications of pregnancy or is unwilling to take the time to use them."

The tragedy is that as the medical indications for abortion receive less acceptance among our best physicians, organized efforts are being made to enlarge the legal authority of doctors to terminate the lives of unborn babies. Sometimes these reasons are alleged to be psychiatric (for example, nervous disorders); eugenic (when there is a danger of a thalidomide baby, for instance); social (too many children already); or economic (poverty). And in these cases a baby's life hinges on a doctor's concept of his ethical responsibility and a social situation. Dr. Alan F. Guttmacher, a spokesman for the Planned Parenthood Federation of America, has admitted: "One is more prone to abort the cardiac patient who is unwed, on relief, and already the mother of several children, than the woman with the same degree of cardiac pathology who is married, childless and well-to-do." Notice how easy it all becomes in the absence of the moral law. Even Dr. Guttmacher agrees that "socio-economic conditions per se never warrant therapeutic abortion." Yet in the Scandinavian countries where abortion has social as well as legal approval, all but a small part of the authorized killings are based on nonmedical grounds.

Sometimes it is argued that easier laws covering "therapeutic" abortions will diminish criminal abortions. The legislature of Denmark accepted that argument in 1939. For the next twelve years there were 5000 legal abortions there a year. But the number of Danish criminal abortions, far from decreasing, increased to 12,000 a year!

Here is where the religious person must stand on the principle that human life is sacred. When such a life is innocent, as the unborn life certainly is, it must remain inviolate. Induced abortion, for whatever reason is a sin of homicide and therefore forbidden. In 1930, Pope Pius XI stated: "It is against the precepts of God and the law of nature: 'Thou Shalt Not Kill.'" This opinion has been held throughout the whole of Christian history and earlier by a long line of Jewish rabbis. One reason the civil law is so severe on this subject is that here is a human life defenseless against attack. Most who favor abortion are unwilling to approve the killing of a child one day after it is born. Yet they would kill the same baby, who prior to birth is helpless.

The doctor, who almost always is a party in the decision to kill, represents the child as well as the mother or the one who pays him. He has the duty to protect both lives. We hear much about the choice between the life of the mother and child as the basic reason for the doctor being the judge over who shall live. Whatever reality existed for such a choice fifty years ago, today one can speak to a whole catalogue of our best obstetricians who admit that they never faced such a choice. And if they should, why should the doctor be judge and jury? If the grounds are not medical, why should not a doctor of sociology make the decision, not a doctor of medicine? And if the grounds are medical, what makes a woman believe that a doctor will always choose her life as the more valuable?

If the mother's life is in such danger that she needs medical or surgical treatment, she should have it—even if the fetus dies as a result. Such indirect deaths occur as a result of hysterectomies and ectopic operations. But where the condition is tuberculosis or hypertension, for example, good medical men reject direct abortion and

work successfully for the life of both. To quote Dr. Guttmacher again: "Modern medicine is a fluid science." If so, the physician's uncertainties are no basis for certain murder.

The following excerpt from a German publication, used effectively by Cardinal Wyszynski of Poland against the efforts of the Polish Government to liberalize the abortion laws, makes its point dramatically.

"October 5: Today my life began. My parents do not know it yet. I am as small as a seed of an apple, but it is I already. And I am to be a girl. I shall have blond hair and azure eyes. Just about everything is settled though, even the fact that I shall love flowers.

"October 19: I have grown a little, but I am still too small to do anything by myself. My mother does just about everything for me. And what is odd—she still doesn't even know that she is carrying me here under her heart, and that she is helping me already, that she is even feeding me with her own blood.

"Some say that I am not a real person yet, that only my mother exists. But I am a real person, just as a small crumb of bread is yet truly bread. My mother is. And I am.

"October 23: My mouth is just beginning to open now. Just think, in a year or so I shall be laughing. I know that my first word shall be—Mama.

"November 2: I am growing a bit every day. My arms and legs are beginning to take shape. But I have to wait a long time yet before those little legs will raise me to my mother's arms, before those little arms will be able to gather flowers and embrace my father.

"November 20: It wasn't until today that the doctor told Mother that I am living here under her heart. Oh, how happy she must be! Are you happy, Mom?

"December 13: I am just about able to see. It is dark around me. When my mother brings me into the world, it will be full of sunshine and flowers. I have never seen a flower, you know. But what I want more than anything is to see my mom. How do you look, Mom?

"December 24: I wonder if Mom hears the whispering beat of my heart? Some children come into the world a little sick. And then the delicate hands of the doctor perform miracles to bring them to health. But my heart is strong and healthy. It beats so evenly—tup-tup, tup-tup . . . You'll have a healthy little daughter, Mom!

"December 28: Today my mother killed me."

Most of those who argue strenuously in favor of abortion believe either that this baby is not human or that his life is not important.

Several research studies have established a direct relationship between criminal abortion and contraception. In 1958 at a seminar on abortion in New York, conducted by the Planned Parenthood Federation of America, Dr. Alfred Kinsey, America's well-known sexologist, insisted that most induced abortions were performed on careless users of contraceptives. How the pattern develops is simple to understand. A couple conclude that they do not want a child. They use contraceptives. If the devices fail and their mind remains set against birth, they next seek abortion, legal or illegal.

Sterilization is the process by which the male or female sex organs are altered surgically so that they cannot do the work of procreation. Performed on the male, the typical operation involves cutting of the *vas deferens*—the duct carrying the sperm cells. This procedure, termed vasectomy, in no way involves the testicles. Performed on the female, the most common method involves tying off the Fallopian tubes, the pathways through which the egg passes from the ovary into the uterus to be fertilized.

Sterilization is in fact a mutilation of the human body. When disease requires surgery to remove ovaries and uterus—thus causing permanent sterility—such mutilation is permissible. The physical well-being of the whole body requires it. But Christians may not maim their bodies at will. We do not possess complete jurisdiction over those bodies. God owns them. We are His stewards and the Fifth Commandment obliges us to protect not only our life but also our physical integrity.

As we commit sin if we take our own lives, so we commit sin if, in the absence of disease, we willfully destroy any part of our bodies. Therefore, it is wrong to perform or accept sterilization when the purpose is not to correct physical deformity, but merely to prevent future births. We may not give away what only God can dispense, even if it would be convenient to do so.

Much is made of sterilization being a voluntary process. But if you saw a man about to jump off a bridge, you would try to stop him. So with sterilization. No one is morally free to sanction its use, even if some human problems might easily be solved thereby.

But people who submit to sterilization are not so free as we might think. Most of such decisions are made under great pressure and usually in a hospital atmosphere. And when we find that most of those who are encouraged to submit to this operation are the poor and members of minority groups, we have reason to question its voluntary aspect as well as its wisdom.

Surgical sterilization has always been condemned in Christian and Hebrew societies. For example, during the 1962 controversy over the sterilization of Negroes in a Virginia hospital, Protestant Evangelist Billy Graham said: "We are in serious danger when we take it upon ourselves to sterilize women even with their consent." Rabbi Jay Kaufman, vice-president of the Union of American Hebrew Congregations, asserted: "Voluntary sterilization unconnected with medical necessity is utterly reprehensible. . . . It is not a necessity, a route of no alternative, merely a convenience."

Nevertheless, the practice is gaining strength, noticeably in Japan and India, and some doctors advocate its wide use in the United States. In most cases, the operation is irreversible. It is highly unlikely that the consenting woman will ever again have children, even if she later changes her mind. The fact that sterilization is generally permanent may make it an ideal technique for dealing with the "population explosion," but hardly less repulsive to people with a Christian view of life.

The very permanency of this operation causes more than a few heartaches. Dr. Guttmacher, himself a devotee of sterilization, has recorded some of these too-late changes of heart:

"A forty-five-year-old Catholic with organic heart disease had a third delivery, her first Caesarian section, at which time her tubes were tied. This gave her a third daughter. She and her husband still want a son.

"A thirty-one-year-old Jewish woman had a third Caesarian section and two living children. Now she wants more children.

"A forty-four-year-old Protestant, the mother of eleven children, sterilized by the removal of the uterus, claims that although she signed permission for the operation, she changed her mind after delivery, but could not make herself understood. So she had the operation against her wishes.

"A twenty-four-year-old Protestant was sterilized after the birth of her sixth living child. Both the patient and her husband now want more children.

"A thirty-six-year-old Protestant was sterilized after having her fourth living child who died of heart disease at the age of eighteen months. She now desires to replace it."

Contraceptionists frequently argue that if married couples use artificial devices to prevent pregnancy, such evils as abortion and sterilization will not be necessary. Evidence to date indicates, however, that the opposite is true —that once the door is opened to contraception by any means, contraception by every means enters as well. Since World War II, Japanese women, although free to use any contraceptive they chose, have elected sterilization and abortion as their favorite methods of preventing births.

The experience of Sweden is equally apropos. In 1938, the Swedes legalized contraception. In 1955, at a Tokyo conference on Planned Parenthood, a spokesman from that Scandinavian land declared: "It has even been admitted that the number of criminal abortions has shown a steady increase since the law came into force. This increase is due to the fact that the possibility of terminating pregnancy has become a common topic of conversation, with the result that the idea of abortion is generally accepted among our people."

In his book, *The Natural History of Population*, Dr. Raymond F. Pearl declared that the number of induced abortions was three to four times greater among those who had used contraception than those who did not. He called abortion "the last desperate remedy to correct the failures of contraceptive techniques." There is probably a similar relationship between contraception and sterilization. One executive of the Planned Parenthood group expounded the wisdom of sterilization in this way: "Then you would not have to be bedeviled with the bothersome use of contraceptives for years, and the attendant fear of birth control failure." In the experience of this writer, pressure is sometimes brought to favor sterilization among those who will not use contraceptives.

In concluding, let us recognize that there will always be women who shut their hearts to everything but their own desires. But many who cry out for abortion at some time during pregnancy when pain and discouragement are hardest, will be profoundly grateful later to those who heeded them not. The old Russian proverb expressed the thought well: "Two small hands upon the breast, and labor is forgotten."

CONSCIENCE AND CONTRACEPTION

Sometimes a person may say: "My conscience is clear. I don't feel bad about using contraceptives (or having an abortion, or submitting to sterilization)." Perhaps the speaker believes what he is saying, but depending entirely upon one's "conscience" is not usually the best way to make a moral decision about the rightness or wrongness of an act.

Many people believe that their conscience is the supreme arbiter of what is good and bad for them. In effect, they are saying that "contraception is right because I say it is."

The error of such thinking becomes clear through an example:

A businessman may have a definite idea of last year's income. Why? Because his reason tells him so. But no tax collector would rely entirely on the taxpayer's honest memory. For this reason, most of us check our records thoroughly before we make a formal statement of our income. We recognize that the truth of falsity of an event does not depend merely on our memory of it or on our statement of it as a fact.

Similarly, when someone says that contraception is good because he thinks it is good, he is merely speaking his mind, not necessarily settling a grave moral issue. But he would be foolish to regard his conscience as the last word. For just as his memory may deceive him, he also may be misled by a false conscience.

He must ask himself: How does my judgment square with that of the Fathers of the Church? With the theologians? And how about the Vicar of Christ on earth? Isn't my possible confusion or uncertainty on moral matters a major reason why God sent the prophets among the Jews and why Christ established the Church?

Nor can "public opinion" on this matter guide the serious-minded religious person. Many examples, down through history, prove that "public opinion" and the moral law are sometimes on different sides. For instance, when Moses proclaimed the Ten Commandments he countered resistance from the crowd, for "public opinion" had good reasons for idolatry. Christ also had conflicts with that group of professional opinion makers, the Pharisees. Man is often weak and the victim of his passions—and organized man can just as easily succumb before organized passion. Public fads can be persuasive in influencing moral judgments on matters like abortion, homosexuality, and genocide, for example, without representing God's truth or moral law.

Contraception is indeed widely practiced in our time. But this proves merely that it is popular—not that it is right. Doctors once believed that it was right to practice craniotomy—the cutting into the head of the fetus to effect delivery. But now all physicians look upon this with horror as a form of baby-killing. Yet the Church condemned craniotomy from the beginning.

In our day, much effort and money has been spent to change men's consciences on questions involving marriage, sex, parenthood, and contraception, and not without substantial success. New doctrines give easy answers by manipulating the natural laws.

Sometimes he fears his own power, however. For example, not long ago a group of scientists told the President of the United States that man is meddling in nature in a frightening way without the remotest idea of how much harm he might cause. These men were talking about polluting the atmosphere by radiation, by polluting water supplies by cutting down forests at a mad pace, and so on.

Contraception also tinkers with the moral order of

man's life. Many people are unconcerned about this, because it appears to solve an immediate problem. But our fathers, and even the fathers and mothers of the present evangelists of contraception, saw things more clearly. Their closeness to nature made them realize that tampering with the marriage act in this way not only offended God, but also harmed themselves and society. The same reason makes it difficult for Planned Parenthood's spokesmen to sell their movement to the Orientals, the Latins, and simple folk everywhere who live close to nature.

But, as the communists have proved, men can be educated to do anything. As regards contraception, the re-education of some moderns has been so complete that they no longer speak a common language with those of us whose way of life remains rooted in natural law and revelation. In the face of a practical problem, what our fathers knew to be wrong has become "right"—as long as it works. Sin has lost all meaning. Nevertheless, we have reason to hope that the universal conscience of men will set present aberrations aright, for as Pope Pius XII declared, "Nature, even if suppressed by violence, always re-asserts itself."

An author of a mathematics text book recommended for his readers this motto: "Be ye doers of the word, not hearers only." He made a wise suggestion. For one does not learn mathematics by learning that mathematical propositions are true, but by working out their proofs. Similarly, man's morality must be something he proves for himself by living out God's law. It is in this moral living that he finds ultimate wisdom and countless arguments against current fads. When a man talks of his conscience on contraception, therefore, he should make sure that it is his true recognition of what God's law actually is (for this is what our real conscience should tell us) and not some man-made brew which has poisoned the soul God gave him.

THE QUESTION OF RESERVATUS

In a separate category as a means of avoiding conception is the practice known as *coitus reservatus* or *amplexus reservatus*. This is a process by which the husband and wife engage in the customary preliminaries of intercourse to the point in which his organ enters her body. The act stops short, however, of the husband's or wife's climax. He does not ejaculate either in the vagina or outside of it. (If he had an orgasm inside the vagina, the action would be an act of natural intercourse. If he withdrew and deliberately ejaculated outside the vagina, the action would be like the one Onan practiced in the Old Testament—the spilling of seed in order to avoid conception. As we have noted, deliberate withdrawal to prevent deposit of the sperm in the vagina is known as *coitus interruptus*. Obviously, too, if the wife reached climax, but the husband did not, this would be masturbation.)

The practice of *coitus reservatus*—literally, reserved copulation—is said to have been developed and used widely by Oriental peoples. It is also reported to be used to some extent among Europeans. Apparently it is not a practice to which Americans in general have become addicted.

Coitus reservatus is highly dubious from any point of

view. It is doubtful practically, unsatisfactory emotionally, and might well be sinful morally.

From the strictly practical point of view, *coitus reservatus* has been described as bringing "brinkmanship" to sex. It calls for extremely great control by the male, a control which physicians say is difficult to achieve without strong motivation and considerable practice. Moreover, it is not uncommon for the penis to secrete semen in advance of the actual orgasm. Consequently, even the rare husband who can stop short of actual ejaculation may have unwittingly deposited sperm in the vagina, making conception possible.

From the emotional point of view, this would seem to be a highly undersirable method of expressing love. It makes it difficult for one, and possibly both partners, to achieve the sense of relief which natural intercourse produces. For many people, this method might well cause greater frustration than if they had refrained from such intense love-making entirely.

It is primarily from the moral point of view, of course, that our objections are based. First, it can lead to the "contraceptive mentality," if it is not in fact a direct result of it. This kind of thinking maintains that pleasure of sex is an end in itself—an attitude that has been strongly condemned by the Popes.

Secondly, it tends to corrupt the entire idea of marriage. Instead of the sex act reflecting the love of both partners—the complete, unrestrained giving of one to the other—the very nature of this technique demands a withholding like that which results from the use of artificial contraceptives. The result is a sense of frustration.

Thirdly, the technique embodies the very danger that

it will lead one or both partners to masturbation. Most men and women have a definite "point of no return" as regards the sexual act. After a certain stage of stimulation has been reached, they experience an almost overwhelming desire to complete the process and to achieve an orgasm. When this is denied in the usual way the temptation to achieve it by solitary means will often be encountered.

5.

The Christian Solution for
These Problems

FOR two thousand years of history since from the time of Our Lord, Christians have always upheld the basic values of family life. Sometimes—as in the days when vice and corruption were rampant in the declining Roman Empire—they had to "fight the good fight" alone. In today's secular world, which has been described as the post-Christian era, again they stand almost alone in defending such ideals as the indissolubility of marriage, the sanctity of married life, and the glory of a parenthood devoted to the duty of teaching children to know, love, and serve God.

As we have seen, many pressures make it extremely difficult, and in cases even impossible, for the Christian husband and wife to have as many children as they might like. About some of these conditions, the individual can do very little but live with them. We are in many ways the creatures of our times. But there are other conditions that he can defeat in their effort to exert a paganizing influence upon him.

To illustrate: The average husband and wife in a large city can do little to change the fact that he is tied to a weekly or monthly salary and must earn his livelihood by working for others. Thus he is dependent upon certain conditions outside his control. If his employer has a slack season, the individual worker has little power of his own to avoid being laid off. Similarly, if he is a factory worker, he has little real power to increase his earning capacity to a substantial degree. Generally, union scales are set so that one will earn about as much as the man next to him. As a union member, a strike or a lockout might keep him off a payroll for weeks at a time.

Nor can one individual do much as a general rule to change his living conditions. For instance, what can he do if landlords habitually refuse to rent apartments to families with children? He can use his political voice to work for adequate government-sponsored housing if private capital cannot or will not provide such accommodations. But achieving this goal through political means is a long, difficult task. The benefits of action by today's husbands and wives probably would be enjoyed only by the next generation.

Perhaps the plight of modern couples would not have become so acute had earlier generations looked ahead and built for the future. And while it may be too late to help today's couples, it is not too late to help tomorrow's. A concern for the future welfare of Christian society is a fitting subject for action by the lay apostolate of today.

The individual Catholic couple need not bow to some

of the other trends in our society. Consider the tendency of wives and mothers to take jobs outside the home. It is often possible for a family to live in reasonable comfort without the mother being forced to take a second job. As a practical matter, her "second income" often adds little to the family's effective spending power. Often it merely keeps her from caring for the children she already has and strongly tempts her to avoid having others.

Most authorities agree that before any couple decide that financial problems can be solved by a wife taking an outside job, or by a husband taking a second one, they should realize that for every additional dollar earned, the income-tax rate will be proportionately higher. Moreover, there will be many extra expenses in connection with the second job. These include costs of traveling to and from work, extra union dues and fees, food at restaurants, etc. Working women generally need more clothing and beauty treatments than do housewives. And working mothers may spend a good part of their earnings on baby sitters and day nurseries to care for their children while they are away. Or they may spend more on transportation and phone calls, trying to co-ordinate their schedules as parents and employees. If they add taxes and the costs of holding a job, they may well find—as does the average working wife—that less than half of every dollar earned is actually added to the family income.

The pressures of "materialism"—the tendency to seek more and more material comforts—may be somewhat more difficult to resist. As we have noted, a basic purpose of advertising is to make consumers dissatisfied with conditions under which they live and to hold out the hope that life will be better if they possess a new car, new refrigerator, new television set, or any one of a thousand other items. If income is spent on all these things, however, there may be little or nothing left to cover the cost of rearing a child.

The younger generation has been exposed to so much advertising from radio, television, billboards, newspapers, magazines, and from other sources, that they have become somewhat resistant to the more strident appeals that are made. Nevertheless, it may be difficult to keep oneself protected against the siren calls of material comfort when one's neighbor on the left sports a new car, the neighbor across the road has new living-room furniture, the one on the right is wearing new clothes, and the one behind is departing for a winter vacation in a warmer climate. It takes careful consideration of the basic purposes of life to conclude that one will do with the things one has, and forego some of the more glittering luxuries that exist all around. Once a husband and wife reach a basic decision and convince themselves that the things money can buy do not of themselves lead to personal satisfaction or lasting happiness, they will be able to set their minds on worth-while goals.

In this connection, it is well to remember that many purchases made by the average family are not really needed, but are made because the old equipment no longer "looks" good. For example, modern automobiles are often replaced after they have run 40,000 miles. It is a fact that the parts of a car that wear out—the motors and tires— can be replaced at a fraction of the cost of a new vehicle. Some owners have operated their cars up to 300,000 miles, replacing parts as needed. Similarly, many household appliances can be made to last fifteen or twenty years instead of being replaced every five years or so when "new" models become irresistible.

The story as regards clothing is much the same. Recently, a man, his wife, and two children moved from San Francisco to New York, where the man's employer assigned him to work for nine months. Time was too short for them to move their household goods, so they simply packed a minimum of clothing in a few suitcases and left several trunkfuls of clothing behind. They soon discovered they could do very well with the limited clothing on hand—that most of their other apparel was actually unnecessary.

It is sometimes surprising to hear the ideas expressed by young couples as to what it takes to succeed in the business world. Some young men seem to be convinced that the employee with expensive clothes and faultless grooming has the best prospects. None will deny the importance of a neat appearance, but it is not necessary to be a "clotheshorse" to succeed. Men who have made their way to the top are often suspicious of those who are too flashy. They would prefer someone who works well and pays more attention to the details of his job. Indeed, most executives would question the prudence of someone who spends an excessive part of his income on his clothing and personal adornment.

Young people also sometimes think it is necessary to entertain lavishly in order to get ahead. This may be true under certain circumstances, but it does not hold in most cases. Equally false is the opinion that it is necessary to drink a great deal. Apart from moral and physical considerations, this habit can be one of the most insidious of all, because the price of mixed drinks in a bar on a given night may equal the cost of feeding a young child for a week. Nevertheless, the idea that heavy drinking is a short cut to success has gained wide credence. In most professions, this is simply not so. Thousands of cases could be cited of men who have lost positions because they drank too much, but it would be difficult to find a case of a man discharged because he did not drink enough.

It is not suggested here, of course, that a couple must strip down to the bare essentials of living. What is being emphasized is that you probably can live comfortably, without sacrificing essential or common luxuries to any considerable extent, by spending less than you may now consider necessary. True, you will not be doing what the Joneses do, but you will have the satisfaction of knowing that you are not blindly following the crowd and are living according to a more solid and satisfying philosophy.

THE ECONOMIC COSTS OF CHILDREN

In modern times, economic pressures are probably the foremost reasons advanced by couples for avoiding conception. As we have seen, economic pressures on the modern wage earner are formidable. And it is indeed true that a baby is costly to bring into the world, and to feed, clothe, and educate until he can support himself. At the same time the difficulties are not so profound as some couples make them. For instance, while the cost of medical care and hospitalization for the expectant mother is high, it can be brought well within reach of the average couple who have been prudent enough to purchase medical and hospital insurance. In fact, the couple who buy this insurance at the outset of their marriage need pay no higher annual premium if they have ten children than if they had none.

In addition, the cost of providing clothing for the baby and such equipment as baby carriages, bassinets, scales, sterilizing equipment, and the like, need not be excessive. Almost everywhere good quality equipment can be bought secondhand at a fraction of its original cost, or can be borrowed from friends or relatives. Nor need it be prohibitively costly, in many cases, to provide a child with food and clothing. He does not need "the best"; for example, inexpensive cuts of meat are just as nourishing as the most expensive ones.

Experts on this subject of family spending maintain that simply by observing a few basic principles, the average couple can save as much as 20 per cent on the necessities of life—often enough to support a child they otherwise could not afford. They can do this by making sure that they do not borrow money at high rates of interest, that they follow a policy, wherever possible, of "cash and carry" shopping, and that they carefully compare prices of different items at different stores. It has been proved, for example, that such items as washing machines and refrigerators often can be bought in one store for $40 or $50 less than in another.

Possibly the greatest error young couples make is that they often fail to realize that their income at age twenty-five will probably be considerably less than the husband will earn in his forties, when the expenses of educating children must be met. Most young men, particularly those working in the so-called white-collar trades, increase their income regularly and reach a peak in their late forties. Not unusually, a man in his late forties earns two or three times as much as he earned at marriage. Even workers in so-called blue-collar fields now enjoy a marked income rise. A young man therefore can count upon earning more money as he grows older, because his increased experience entitles him to it.

Thus it would be a mistake for a couple in their twenties to decide that they cannot afford a child because they could not send him to college on the husband's salary. Moreover, parents should not overlook the fact that it is becoming easier and easier for talented young people to obtain college educations, because more and more scholarships are being offered every year. It can be truthfully said that any young man or woman who could benefit from a college education and truly wants one can achieve his goal through systems of aid and by working part time. Parents sometimes worry about their ability to send their child to college, but if the child himself is determined, he generally can achieve this objective by himself and without outside aid.

WHAT ARE A COUPLE'S "REAL REASONS?"

Psychology teaches us that the reasons people give for doing or not doing certain things may not be the real reasons or may be only partial ones. Deep in the subconscious may be hidden fears, desires, and ambitions which influence a person's desire to do certain things.

This is not to say that persons tell an untruth deliberately when they advance other motives. Often, they are but dimly aware of their real motives. This is also true in cases of persons deciding whether to have a child.

Becoming a parent is a monumental step—certainly one of the most important in any person's life. It involves the decision to be responsible for the child's moral, emotional, and physical welfare until he is old enough to care for himself. When a young man and woman think about becoming parents, they cannot help but be influenced subconsciously by their own experiences as children, by the experiences of their mothers and fathers as parents, as well as by all the things they have heard and read about the subject. Sometimes a child's single experience may tilt the scales in his attitude towards parenthood.

When a couple decide that they do not want a child, they may have perfectly legitimate and valid reasons for their decision. As we shall see in Chapter 7, these reasons may be of a physical, economic, eugenic, or social nature. In fact, any serious difficulty that might result from the pregnancy may exempt a couple from parenthood, provided that they avoid conception by abstaining from intercourse when the wife is fertile.

Nevertheless, couples sometimes decide that they do not want children when, in fact, they are fully capable of bringing them into the world and supporting them without any danger to health. When such a couple sincerely advance reasons against having babies, they might well ask themselves whether or not motives beneath the surface may be influencing their decision.

An attractive young bride, the child of well-to-do parents, who was married to a man with excellent prospects, appeared in a psychiatrist's office to seek treatment. She said that she was unable to give herself freely and without reservation to her husband in the marriage act. She could not understand why she always resisted his approaches. After a few frank conversations, it developed that the girl's mother, from her earliest days, had stressed the importance of retaining an attractive face and figure in order to be appealing to men. This girl had come to believe that personal beauty was the most important possession. Moreover, she had the fixed notion that pregnancy would make her fat, ugly, and repulsive to her husband. This was a calamity to be avoided at all costs.

She realized, of course, that such a fear was unjustified, but it persisted nevertheless. Rather than acknowledge it openly, she gave as her reason for avoiding childbirth that she was too high strung to stand the strain of caring for a young baby.

It was then the psychiatrist's function to point out that most women become more attractive to their husbands when they are pregnant, at least in a spiritual sense, because their husbands realize that they are doing a noble work of bringing their own children into the world. It is a fact, of course, that most husbands are more considerate of their wives during pregnancy than at any other time. When the psychiatrist spoke to the wife and her husband together, the latter said that his wife would be more attractive as a mother than as a mere childless companion.

The young bride's fears diminished when they were brought out into the open and dealt with in an intelligent way—as did her reasons for avoiding pregnancy. She now has two children and her unjustified fears of motherhood have vanished. She is completely responsive to her husband in their marital relations as a result.

Another wife had become prematurely gray in her early twenties after the birth of her second child. At first, she was convinced that premature grayness was a mark of distinction, for everyone commented upon how attractive she looked. As a result, she never bothered to dye her hair as many women do.

After a while, however, she began to feel that her gray hair made her look much too old. She also became more and more vehement in objecting to her husband's suggestion that they have a third child. At first, she said that they could not afford a baby although persons in their own set, with a considerably lower income, were managing nicely with four or five. Once, in a spirited conversation, she let slip her real reason. "How would it look," she asked, "to have an old gray-haired woman wheeled into the delivery room? Everybody would laugh at me."

Tactfully, the husband suggested that the wife visit a hairdresser. When the wife ceased to be gray-haired, became a brunette, and looked her real age, she began to think of herself as a young woman again, and was ready for childbearing.

Despite his wife's desire for many children, a young husband insisted that it was impossible to support even one child on his earnings, even though others in his income bracket had several children without apparent strain. Only after many discussions did his wife discover his real reason. As a youngster in a family of three he had often witnessed his parents' battles over money matters. He vividly remembered his mother complaining that she was unable to maintain a household on the amount his father provided, and his father protesting vigorously whenever his children needed new shoes.

This young man grew up believing that a child was nothing but an economic burden, and he was determined never to worry about family expenses. He realized, of course, that most grownups manage to bring children into the world and to feed and educate them without grave crises. Rather than admit his real reasons, however, he expressed a point of view which made him appear like a devoted provider who wished to give every advantage to his child.

In another case, a young bride advanced many reasons for avoiding pregnancy, but one of the real ones was the fact that she would feel "ashamed" of being seen in a pregnant condition. As a child, she had often noticed young boys laughing at the sight of a woman with child, and she had also seen people turn and stare at a pregnant woman. Her mother did not help matters by indicating that sex was "not nice." The girl decided that there was something shameful in pregnancy, and that the only practical choice was between remaining indoors during the period of visible pregnancy so that no one could ridicule her, or of refusing to become pregnant. She chose the latter course.

It took a long discussion with a priest to make her realize that pregnancy, rather than being a condition for ridicule, should actually be a cause for pride. The priest pointed out that anyone who holds an expectant mother up to ridicule obviously holds wrong attitudes. The priest then explained that the notion that sex is "not nice" undoubtedly stems from the idea that intercourse itself is evil. This idea ignores the fact that sex is the means God devised to perpetuate the human race, and that all the saints of the Church came into the world through inter-course.

It should also be pointed out that the desire for a large family may sometimes be motivated by less than worthy reasons. In one case, the oldest of four sons had always been an indifferent student. He had found him-self in several scrapes with school authorities and even with the police.

While he could obtain no better job than as an un-skilled worker, his brothers were entering the professions. One became a lawyer, another an accountant, a third a teacher. The oldest child resented their success and was determined to "show them up." Although he could not afford a large family, and was not disposed to give his youngsters the fatherly care and attention they deserved, he entered a race to produce as many children as possible. When his thirteenth was born, he boasted that he was "a better man than all his brothers put together." Such an ambition, of course, is hardly a proper one.

Another man has a wife whose doctor strongly advised her not to have another baby. The husband insisted upon intercourse during her fertile period nonetheless. Another couple know that they cannot afford more children, but they were too stupid or selfish to control themselves. Naked lustfulness such as theirs sometimes is the explana-tion for large families of parents who really should not have them.

The subject of why people think and act as they do is much too deep and complicated for discussion in this book. But it would be well for every couple to realize that their attitudes towards parenthood may not withstand the light of Christian ideals.

We might also keep in mind that it is quite easy for a couple to develop excuses for avoiding parenthood once they set their minds to it. Let us assume that a couple decide for purely selfish reasons that they do not want a child. Once their decision is made, they develop excuses that are more appealing than those based upon sheer selfishness. They put out high-sounding reasons (which they may even believe after a while) to cover an action which is disreputable in itself. Even criminals often convince themselves that they are somehow performing a service to humanity.

It has always been possible to postpone parenthood on the ground that "these are no proper times to bring a child into the world." In fact, a husband and wife now in their fifties could have been able to find excuses throughout their childbearing period to avoid pregnancy. When they were married in the 1930s, the world was in the midst of a severe economic depression. Millions were unemployed and pessimists were doubting that prosperity would ever return. In the latter part of the thirties, war clouds were moving over the horizon. In 1938, Hitler moved to Sudetenland, and prophets were generally predicting that world war would break out before long. On September 1, 1939, the war did, in fact, begin. It lasted until 1945. Of course, a couple then could find a "perfect" excuse: Who would want to bring a baby into a world at war?

The end of the war opened an era of unparalleled prosperity—the ideal time for having children, judging by depression-day objections, but by then those who wished to do so did not have to look far for other reasons to avoid parenthood. First, there were prophecies of a world-wide depression, similar to the postwar economic difficulties that had followed World War I, and then there was the fact of the atomic bomb. When relations between the Western powers and Russia grew worse, and Russia herself developed nuclear weapons, the world again faced the serious danger of war. This danger exists today—and we are back where we started.

A couple married in the 1930s who used these excuses to avoid having children would now face a possibly bitter, lonely old age. The woman who refused to have children during her fertile years because "the times were out of joint" now would have no children to comfort her and, in fact, would face old age knowing that through her own fault she has not achieved fulfillment as a woman. Nor would her husband feel that he had expressed his manhood and known the satisfactions that come only from fatherhood.

On the other hand, couples who courageously had children in the depressed and "dangerous" thirties and during the war years, now have children and grandchildren to comfort them.

Whenever a couple disagree about whether or not to have children, they might well spend a little time in quiet, prayerful thought, without emotionalism if possible, in trying to determine what is a reasonable attitude to take. It may often be found that their basic motives, if brought to the surface, can be dispelled through reason and knowledge. On the other hand, their motives may be entirely pure, even praiseworthy. Furthermore, there is no obligation to do the gravely inconvenient.

Suppose a young bride has a mother who has continually complained about the horrible difficulties of having and raising children. Or suppose that in her own childhood days, a relative or friend had a difficult delivery. She may have excessive fears of the hazards of pregnancy. But if she will think about things calmly, she will realize that most dangers have gone out of childbearing and that there is every likelihood that she will give birth to a normal, healthy baby. In fact, doctors state without qualification that the woman who consults an obstetrician as soon as she suspects pregnancy, and who arranges to have her baby delivered in a hospital, virtually assures herself of safety.

If a husband or wife persist in attitudes toward parenthood which the other thinks are unjustified by facts, they might ask an experienced marriage counselor to help them resolve their problem. The local pastor may be able to provide a perspective which one or the other may lack. Often another level-headed married couple can be greatly helpful. Probably in every parish there are older husbands and wives who have been "through the mill" themselves and can give sound down-to-earth counsel. They know that devoted young couples can outlive most problems.

It may be necessary to consult a psychologist or psychiatrist to reach the real reasons at the root of their disagreement. It would be well, however, to consult a professional counselor who sympathizes with the Catholic position regarding family-planning. Some psychiatrists unfortunately hold the view that artificial contraception is the way to cure most problems of this type, giving little thought to its effect upon the spiritual well-being of the parties involved.

HOW THE CHRISTIAN SOLUTION DIFFERS

When all this has been said, the fact remains that there probably are times in every Christian marriage when it becomes necessary to avoid conception for short or long periods. As we shall see in Chapter 7, Pope Pius XII enumerated the conditions under which couples may be excused from the obligation of parenthood for periods lasting up until the very life of their marriage. These conditions are based upon humane considerations for the welfare of the family as a whole, the health of the mother, and the dignity of both parents and children.

But whereas the Church teaches that the avoidance of children may be necessary or desirable at times, two important distinctions must be made. For the Christian solution differs in both motivation and technique from that of the contraceptionists.

In motivation: because a Christian man and woman enter marriage with the desire to have more than an isolated experience with parenthood, taking into consideration the health and well-being of the mother, the father's ability to support them, and the prospects of a good family life in an environment which enables the children to make use of the talents which God gives them. When the Christian concludes, after prayerful thought, that it is not possible or feasible to conceive a child, the decision is made on a note of genuine sadness because the parents are to lose the opportunity to become co-creators with God of a precious human life.

In technique: the difference is even more marked. For while contraceptionists hold in effect that any method may be used to prevent conception, the Christian solution states that the husband and wife abstain from intercourse on such days when it is likely to result in conception. The contraceptionist uses artificial means to defeat the purposes which God intended. On the other hand, the Christian does not engage in the act at all when he believes that conception might occur. When he engages in the sex act on "safe" days, he merely makes use of a means which God Himself created. He is not "improving upon God," as if such were possible.

Those who subscribe to the notion that "the easy way is always best" may argue that it is difficult for a man and woman to abstain from sexual relations when they must do so if conception is to be avoided. One cannot deny that abstention requires more will power and a greater willingness to make sacrifices than does submission to passion. Sometimes abstention may be extremely difficult—for instance, when a couple must refrain for prolonged periods. But it is absurd to say—as many "moderns" do—that what is difficult is also impossible. In fact, we know that abstention can be achieved even for the lifetime of a marriage. When practiced for good reasons, and when a couple have a clear idea of the purposes of their marriage, the nature of their love for each other and the nature of the sexual appetite itself, they will better understand why "periodic abstinence" is not only possible but is also an absolute necessity at times, and why the person who will not practice it is inevitably headed toward personal disaster.

Let us, then, examine the very nature of sex in marriage.

6.

The Place of Sex in Marriage

"WHAT can I do with my husband?" constantly ask wives who do not want more babies. If they were more honest, they would ask: "What can I do with sex?"

These are not small questions. One woman told me: "A couple should do what is natural. You put two people in the cozy proximity of the marriage bedroom, which most of us economically and socially can never abandon, and you ask almost the impossible in most cases." Another wife said: "Does it seem likely that a couple in love are going to base what God intended to be a spontaneous giving of themselves on the regulation of a calendar?"

These are not bad women nor bad Catholics. If they were, we could ask why they think that doing what comes naturally under any and all circumstances is necessary or good. But because they already have manifested willingness to use the sexual faculties reasonably, their protests merely reflect dissatisfaction with some of the tension associated with living a sexual life without sex.

Recurring in all of these complaints is a commonly held belief that the sexual life of any married couple follows a natural rhythm which must be allowed expression. According to this opinion, to thwart the spontaneous upsurge of sexual passion is unnatural, and creates a peril to the conjugal union itself. Usually, husbands are used as evidence to support this point of view, although aggressive females sometimes outshine men in sexual vigor.

Admittedly, if one lives in a culture which accepts this viewpoint as gospel, there are difficulties. Fertile women begin to envy sterile women, and some husbands develop animosity to the so-called frigid wives. Associated with this attitude also are infidelity, contraceptive love, even homosexuality. We do not wish to diminish the importance of these problems nor deny that they exist. We are where we live and most of us tend to make right what our neighbors believe to be right, particularly if enjoyment is the reward.

While the married couple confined to a bedroom at night are in a class by themselves, it might be proper to point out that the same argument of "rhythm in sexual drives" or "spontaneity in love" is being used by engaged couples, even by teen-agers, to justify premarital intercourse, although obviously, the married would say, with no real justification.

Unquestionably, too, as far as men are concerned, God has endowed them with a very natural aptitude for sexual relations and has filled their bodies with creative elements that call for union. Far more than women, their bodies seek satisfaction. And while it is sometimes alleged that during fertile times of the month women are equally in "heat," this so far is an unsubstantiated hypothesis. We do know, however, that sex, if by that we mean the urge to union with a member of the opposite sex, is natural and good, but a matter of mind as well as body. Sensualists make a great joke about celibates, and even Catholics think that the Christian doctrine on sex is the result of celibate thinking (even bringing Our Lord within their condemnation). But the existence of celibacy—and successful celibacy at that— among pre-Christian Jews, among Buddhists, and obviously among Catholic priests, brothers, and nuns—is proof positive that sexual energy is often directed (the psychiatric term is "sublimated") to higher purposes and is thereby controlled. The Christian praise of the consecrated virgin is not merely approval given to a higher life but a vindication of the reasonableness of conjugal chastity.

No one can argue that the problems of married couples sleeping in the same house are small, not only because they are ordained to sexual union, but because they are two people who may want to live by different values. Sometimes the disagreement has nothing to do with sex but reflect his willingness to repeat his fatherhood, if need be, and her unwillingness. Or vice versa. Once the answer to a new pregnancy is "No," all sorts of chain reactions set in. And the sexual area may well become the first battleground with fighting at times open, at other times subtle and devious.

It is here that every couple must sit down and think, particularly if they are Christians and have any respect for the place assigned by God and Christ to sex within and without marriage.

Sex is as old as the human race and living with one's sexual drives is neither a new problem nor one peculiar to moderns. Throughout history men and women, mostly men, have had to deal with powerful appetites for each other, implanted in them by no less a Person than Almighty God Himself. Sex may not be as important as life, but, granting this exception, there is no urge in man more basic and more conducive to happiness or unhappiness.

There is much mystery in our sexuality. Why did God make man male and female? Most of us spend a lifetime finding out; others after half a century learn nothing. So many elements of nature are mixed together. Man wants woman. Woman is willing to take him. Man comes to sex with far more emphasis on the physical experience. But to woman, receiving a man is not merely accommodation to the sensual; her love, as the pleasure which follows, is more total and pervasive. Because it is so instinctive, man's sexual love can be devoid of spirit. But woman seeks more than ecstasy. She seeks the approval of her man and the fruit of union which is children. Someone has said that every woman who truly gives herself to man wants his child. This is true. And by that fact it is her wantonness which corrupts sexuality.

The free spirit of man makes him undiscriminating in his sex objects. Woman, through history and, apart from the Church, almost alone, subjugates her lord and master by binding him to marriage, fidelity, and parenthood. He who struts proudly in fatherhood learned his magnificence only by the total giving of her motherhood. She,

for whom sex is almost a secondary characteristic because
it is so internal and spiritual, teaches him the divine purposes of sex. What a shame then when she becomes more
anxious about the moment and less about the eternal!

Life's puzzle, certainly the meaning of sex, is not
always easy to unravel without help. Here are two different human beings, endowed with varying interests and
needs, prevented from fulfillment by different fears, joined
by God in the ineffable union of marriage. At a young
age mostly, and driven there by forces hardly understood,
they are led by God to undertake a great adventure—the
making of men—and this means much more than conception. To do this divinely appointed work, husbands and
wives must use their talents, including their sexuality. Sex,
like a brain or a strong right arm, is a real talent, a real
passion, a real power, but one less reasonable than a brain
and harder to control than a strong right arm.

In man's case, however, this is not an animal power
that demands satisfaction merely by the asking. Sometimes people make it so and the more they are removed
from religion the more it is so. Human sex is suffused
with human spirit. It is man's mind, rather than his body,
which tells him how to use it. It is his will which makes
him its master or its slave. A sexual life between a mother
and a son, living in equally close quarters, is abhorrent
even to the pagan and between brother and sister hardly
less so. Unfaithful married love may merit the attention
of scenario writers but in real life it breaks human hearts
and destroys human families. Homosexuality for either
men or women may be sickness but more likely depravity.

Original sin has left its mark on man, on both sexes.
Man is not as smart as he should be, nor as strong. And

successive eons of Adam's children, particularly those
brought up outside the Jewish and Christian tradition,
demonstrate too well how weak man is when he is dominated by sex. In all ages of history men have attempted
to separate sex from marriage and sex from parenthood,
because sex is pleasant, while marriage and parenthood
are not always pleasant. It is so very human to gravitate
toward what comes easily. Conversely, it takes real spirituality to subordinate flesh to spirit. People like David
and Solomon, places like Sodom and Gomorrah, were
called to judgment by God precisely for the abuse of
their sexual powers. In turn God sent the Jewish prophets,
His only Begotten Son, and now the Church to remind
men, among other things, that in the use of sex He expects more of them than He does of animals. For God,
sex is a creature to be used and to be dominated. This
means that for God, sex is related both to marriage and
parenthood.

When God created man, He could have made him sex-
less. All things are possible for God. Most certainly, He
could have devised a way of creating man continuously
without a second sex. A tree, for example, drops its seed,
and the processes of nature do the rest. In early forms,
life simply divides its cells and new life appears. But God
decided to make man and give him a woman. This was a
deliberate decision, one which He did not have to make.
But He made it and certainly for a purpose.

Man and woman, by Divine Design, are alike in
many particulars. Their basic bodily functions are similar. Their sight, hearing, senses of taste, touch, and smell
are fundamentally the same. Both must eat the same
kinds of food to nourish their bodies. They walk and talk

in the same basic fashion. When a child is born, one cannot tell from looking at the face or general outline of the body whether it is a boy or girl. The only way to detect the difference is by observing the organs of sex.

This difference in the sex organs and in inherent physical and emotional qualities are the basic points of difference between men and women. But note: These differences pertain directly to the qualities that men and women require in order to procreate and provide for new generations of mankind. The sex organs are different because God has decided that participation by both the male and female are necessary before a child can be conceived. And the emotional qualities are different: Men have general qualities that enable them to be providers for their families—to supply the food that the family needs; women generally have the tenderness, affection, concern for the welfare of others, that enable them to do a better job of caring for children.

Thus, God consciously created the basic qualities of mind, body, and spirit to enable man to be a father and woman to be a mother. And in creating two sexes, He created the idea of marriage—the means by which man and woman would unite, not only in body but also in heart and mind, to provide the setting into which children might be born and educated to know Him and serve Him.

When God created the first marriage, He spoke to mankind when He said, "Increase and multiply and fill the earth." (Genesis, 1:28.) From these words which He spoke to Adam and Eve, it is clear that His basic idea was for man and woman to unite in marriage for the purpose of having and caring for children. He also made it possible for husbands and wives to engage in the act of sex as a way of cementing their mutual love and of providing comfort and satisfaction for each other. That God had this other purpose may be inferred from the fact that He said that, "It is not good for man to be alone." He obviously intended the second sex to complete man—to be complementary to him. In His plan, man and woman would be united in marriage so that they could provide love for each other, companionship, and affection. It is the duty of husband and wife to help each other to reach spiritual and emotional fulfillment, and to move toward their ultimate destiny, now as a couple. And this means love—real love.

WHAT IS MARRIED LOVE?

To love another really, one must be willing to love the whole man or woman—heart, mind, soul, as well as body. Love at its best is a spiritual experience, not merely an emotional or physical one. It is spiritual because personal convenience or personal needs are put last. A mother's love for her newborn babe is the most obvious example of that. Examine the life story of the world's great lovers, mostly the saints, and you find that they loved whole and entire, not merely a part or a side of man. For them the needs of the soul take precedence over the needs of the body. In romantic love, on the other hand, you will find large doses of selfishness and sensuality.

As the Catholic marriage ritual says: "We are willing to give in proportion as we love. And when love is perfect, the sacrifice is complete. God so loved the world that He gave His only begotten Son; and the Son so loved us that He gave Himself for our salvation. Greater love than this no one has, than a man lay down his life for his friends."

Husbands and wives do not grow to this kind of love overnight. Certain inequalities exist between the two at all times, one loving more, one loving less, the husband more casual, the wife more spiritual. For many couples, however, time and sharing produce that more perfect union.

But even when the defects of personality or the difficulty of real life situations make the realization of ideal love unobtainable, God ordains the couple to a minimum of love, that which they are bound to give whether they like it or not. The married state is God's invention and so His law prescribes minimum standards of behavior so that His purposes will be realized, apart from the shortcomings of the parties themselves. And so we have the moral law of marriage covering such things as the oneness of marriage, the indissoluble bond, fidelity, sex relations, procreation, chastity, and so forth.

The world does not look upon love this way, but this is the kind of love that gives, as the Church's marriage ceremony tells us, "The greatest measure of earthly happiness that may be allotted to man in this vale of tears." And even when the "greatest measure" is unobtainable on earth, there are the eternal rewards for a job well done under trying circumstances. In the meantime, family life itself is protected from disintegration (as we see going all around us) by the insistence on God's minimum requirements.

While Christian people make the best of what they

got, even a bad lot, there is no reason why they should not use all of their abilities to work through their difficulties and improve the quality of the love. Most of the complainers in marriage would complain regardless of the situation, simply because they are incapable of real love, never grew up, or reject Christ's gospel for the married.

In order to strengthen your love for your marriage partner, you should strive to understand his or her nature so that you may better satisfy his or her spiritual and emotional needs. If you try to understand your mate's personality—the general characteristics of the sex as well as individual idiosyncrasies—you will help yourself to accept or adjust to them. Acceptance of your mate's characteristics is important, because both the sexes, and the individuals who comprise them, are different in many important particulars. For example, a woman by nature tends to be tender, loving, "soft-hearted." In her everyday relationships, her actions reflect these qualities. By nature, a man tends to be more dynamic, aggressive, and authoritative, and less inclined towards tenderness.

It is important for the growth of love that the husband recognize that his wife does things that he either would not do or would do in a different way, simply because her nature and training are different from his. Similarly, a wife should strive to understand that many things her husband does differently also reflect his masculine nature and the training he has received to fit him for a man's world.

From understanding and acceptance grows the greatest of all aids to marital harmony and love—the quality of charity, for in charity there is a positive desire to do what is necessary for the fulfillment of a partner's needs.

Therefore, the devoted husband and wife will constantly seek to do that which is in the best interests of the other. To the extent that a man or woman turns from his or her own selfish desires, will he or she achieve the true dimensions of love.

Because we have physical needs as well as spiritual and emotional ones, the act of sex is one of the ways in which a husband and wife can express their love. But— and this is most important—it is only one of many ways by which this can be done.

Many moderns apparently think that the words "sex" and "love" are synonymous. Nothing could be farther from the truth, and probably no idea could do greater harm to the Catholic couple seeking to perfect themselves in marriage.

A little thought will convince us that it is entirely possible for a husband and wife to achieve a high level of mutual love if need be, without recourse to sex, and that it is often when sex is renounced for a short period or even permanently, that the highest levels are indeed reached.

The ideal of Christian family life is the Holy Family of Jesus, Mary, and Joseph. No one could say that Joseph's love for Mary was an inferior love. In fact, the protection and direction which he provided is a model for every Christian husband. In this household, there was love on the highest level of self-sacrifice that human beings can achieve. Yet, as we are told, the Blessed Mother remained a virgin throughout her life. Joseph had marital rights by virtue of his marriage to Mary but did not choose to use them because of his reverence for God. Although the love between Mary and Joseph was a virginal one, this did not detract in any way from its quality.

While Mary and Joseph were unique, examples of love without sex can readily be found among ordinary people. One of the most touching of scenes is that of the husband or wife who cares for an invalid mate, cheerfully giving of self for long periods when sexual union is impossible. Often a husband will display the most tender actions of which he is capable during the latter stages of his wife's pregnancy, or after she has returned home with her newborn baby—times when, for medical reasons, intercourse is prohibited.

When practiced for good motives, abstinence is actually a higher form of love. It contains more of the basic ingredients of love—the willingness to sacrifice temporary satisfactions for a higher purpose. Abstinence properly motivated is a denial of self, while the act of sex usually has some element, however small, of taking. Therefore the practice of the virtue of chastity is the practice of self-sacrifice upon which true love is built.

On the other hand, suppose a wife becomes seriously ill, and her doctor orders her to remain in bed quietly, taking powerful medicines if she is to be cured. At such a time her husband approaches and demands intercourse. Would such a relationship be an act of love? Of course not; instead it would be an experience in selfishness repulsive to normal men and women. It would totally lack the sense of charity and consideration for the welfare of the other person that is the cornerstone of love.

Or suppose a husband habitually regards the marital act as one devised for his pleasure solely. He makes no effort to help his wife in achieving the release of her own sexual tensions. He is one of those benighted men—of whom there are still some—who think that sex is a masculine prerogative to enjoy, and that it is "not nice" for a woman to derive pleasure from it. When he looks upon his wife as a mere instrument to gratify his own appetite, he obviously is not motivated by idealistic motives. Rather he is engaging in selfish indulgence. He is taking, not giving—and that is the very opposite of the spirit of love.

Unless used in the proper way, sex in fact can be a means not toward the cementing of love, but rather toward its direct opposite. Consider the tragic wretch who walks the streets of big cities, offering to sell her body to anyone with the price. When she and her patron submit to an act of sex, is it "love" they engage in? Or, at the end of the experience, is not its purchaser filled with a loathing for the act he has committed, and is she not degraded by it?

Overemphasis on the importance of sex in marriage can be the means of ruining the marriage itself. One sees vivid examples of this in the highly publicized marriage histories of actors and actresses. Some of these actresses are advertised as the most sexually desirable women on earth, and they devote hours of every day to making themselves as sexually appealing as possible. If sex were all there is to love, they should achieve the most stable and lasting marital relationships. But the contrary is often true. Their marriages, when contracted on the basis of physical attraction and with little emotional or spiritual foundation, often flounder within a few years, if not within months.

We can see, therefore, that a mere physical union between man and woman, no matter how physically attractive, is no guarantee that a sense of mutuality and love will result. But when a husband and wife perform the marital act with a desire to provide that which is good for his or her mate, and to satisfy the other partner, it is essentially an act of giving—and therefore an act of love.

Of course, the normal young man and woman entering marriage have strong sexual instincts and intercourse can serve to strengthen their love for each other and release their physical tensions. But it would be a mistake to assume that love on a high level could not be achieved if sex were denied to them for a time. True, the sexual act smooths the road to true love among husband and wife. But the road can be traversed—even if with difficulty—without it.

Now consider the case of a young couple who have decided that they should not have a baby at this time. They know that the use of contraceptives is evil, and they also know that there are only several days in each month when a woman can become pregnant—that on other days intercourse performed in a natural way will not result in conception. What course must they follow? They may abstain from intercourse on those days on which they might conceive a child. This is periodic continence. This is an exercise in the Virtue of Conjugal Chastity.

CHASTITY IS FOR EVERYONE

There is much confusion about chastity. In our society it is not popular, even among the single. It is not uncommon for today's Don Juan to solicit his girl friend with the question: "What are you saving yourself for?" as if not having sexual relations is somewhat old-fashioned or abnormal. As bad as that state of mind is, the assumption that chastity is something for the unmarried only, is equally erroneous.

The fact of the matter is: Chastity is that moral virtue which enables all of us, single or married, to use our sexual powers rightly. And it is important that we do all things rightly. The virtue of temperance, for example, empowers us to eat and drink what we need to live, tells us not to consume harmful foods and liquids, inhibits us from eating too much or too little. When it comes to regulating our sexual appetites, this same virtue of temperance is necessary for a good moral life. Only now we call it chastity.

Chastity, therefore, is the virtue which commands us when to use and not use our sexual powers, tells us whom we may or may not love sexually, and indicates how these faculties should be used intelligently and reasonably, as God would wish them used.

Chastity commands different things for the married, as distinguished from the single. Unmarried men and women may not deliberately seek sexual satisfaction at all. But husbands and wives are most chaste when they use their marital rights properly. Chastity, then, does command sexual love. Men and women in marriage are expected to use sex as a means of strengthening their affection. A woman, for example, who refuses her husband, not only offends justice but chastity as well. And the husband who exercises his marital rights crudely or brutally, is equally unchaste, as is an unfaithful spouse. So chastity is not sexlessness, but the right use of sex.

But in some instances the right use of sex (chastity) means that these powers will not be used. This surprises no one. Wives get sick, become pregnant, and husbands are away from home on business.

Most of the complaining comes, however, when the couple decide not to have another baby. One husband, the father of six, made this comment: "Since the birth of our last child three years ago, I wait for my wife to let me know when marital relations will be safe. Loving her dearly, I could ask for no more." Would that more couples were that chaste. Unfortunately, too many look upon marriage as a playground for sexual energy. Secular marriage manuals call for unlimited titillation of the senses so that continence becomes robbery.

Many persons apparently believe that the sexual appetite must be appeased whenever it manifests itself, even if it manifests itself under forced stimulation. According to this thinking, control of one's sexual appetites is unnatural, and chastity for the married can lead to great dangers. It is the theory of some psychiatrists, for example, that mental health results from giving in to instincts that arise—that the control of one's appetites somehow leads to neurosis. But as Erich Fromm has commented in his book, *The Art of Loving*, "the obvious clinical facts demonstrate that men—and women—who devote their lives to unrestricted sexual satisfaction do not attain happiness, and very often suffer from severe neurotic conflicts or symptoms. The complete satisfaction of all instinctual needs is not only not a basis for happiness; it does not even guarantee sanity." This should be obvious.

Consider a man who has never learned to control his passions. At the slightest temptation—for example, the sight of a sexy photograph in a newspaper or of a provocative woman on the stage or screen—a desire for sex is aroused, encouraged, and satisfied. Who could possibly argue that such an individual was trained to lead any kind of responsible, mature life? In truth, the person in the modern world who has not learned to control his sexual desires—in view of the constant bombardment of sexual stimulation thrown at him from all sides—will literally become a complete slave to passion.

To take another example, consider the young girl who gives in to every instinct of passion and succumbs to every male who approaches her. What are her prospects for marital happiness? Certainly the husband of such a woman would be unable to count on her fidelity as soon as she left his sight. The need for self-control is so obvious that it is one of the great mysteries of our time that there should be any question about it.

In fact, one can say with absolute certainty that the marriage without chastity is a marriage doomed. For there are countless times in the life of every married couple—entirely apart from moral considerations—when they will have to curb their desires and abstain from intercourse. For example, there will be times when the husband or wife is ill. Such illnesses may extend for a few days, or even for months. Suppose a wife argued that she was entitled to copulate with another man because her own husband was unable to engage in sexual relations for several months. Even secularists of the worst kind would frown on her action and tell the husband he was entitled to divorce her under such circumstances.

On other occasions, either or both parties will be emotionally upset, perhaps worried over the illness of a child, parent, relative, or friend, and not in the mood to give himself or herself freely in intercourse. For instance, would it not be an unfeeling husband who would insist on relations when his wife's mother lay on her deathbed?

At other times, the husband and wife may be separated for days, months, or even years. A man is suddenly called to duty with the Armed Forces. He is sent to a distant country where his wife cannot join him. Would he sanction an act of adultery—a lack of chastity by his wife under such circumstances? Would she condone his unchastity in the distant land? The answer is obvious.

During her childbearing period, a woman sometimes is told by her doctor to abstain from intercourse during the early months of pregnancy, during the last six weeks of it, and also for at least several weeks after childbirth. Thus the husband may be required to practice abstinence for as long as a month and a half continuously. In addition, for four or five days out of every month, when a wife is menstruating, one or both partners may have esthetic objections to intercourse. Abstention at this time is not necessary, but many couples impose it voluntarily. And they think nothing of it. They do not maintain the attitude that they are being deprived of some great privilege or that they are undergoing great suffering on those days.

Men and women expect continence of their mates under circumstances such as those outlined above, and they do not think they are imposing exceptional or unbearable burdens when they do so. For instance, a wife would be justifiably disturbed if, during the last stages of her pregnancy or when she was in the hospital giving birth, her husband were unwilling to practice sexual abstinence. Or a husband would be justified in his anger if his wife would not control her passions when he was forced to be away from home on a business trip.

Even the atheistic communists recognize the need for periodic abstinence in marriage, for they still exact a pledge of fidelity of husbands and wives, implying that during the periods of absence and illness that every couple know, the satisfaction of the sex appetite outside of marriage is not to be tolerated. The promise made by brides and bridegrooms in the civil marriage ceremony in East Germany, reads as follows:

"To all workers: We swear to make our marriage, entered into here today, a community for life. . . . We swear to respect one another; to give one another every solicitude, aid and sacrifice which may be necessary; to help one another in the interests of our professional and cultural development; to conform to this ideal in all our decisions *and to be unfailingly faithful to one another.*"

What makes abstinence easy for most men and women under the circumstances described above is that they are acting with the proper motivation. It is a fact that idealism makes chastity less difficult—that abstinence for a good purpose is possible and laudable. Furthermore, when a husband and wife fully understand why they must abstain from sex, they are much more capable of doing so. And this abstention, it must be stressed, is on a purely natural level. Men and women without religious beliefs, but simply with an ordinary sense of decency, are capable of doing it. How much easier, then, can it be for husbands and wives motivated by a love of God and who, thanks to the sacrament of marriage, can draw on Divine grace to help them.

The importance of motivation was illustrated recently

by a young businessman whose employer required him to take frequent four- and five-day trips away from his home. This young man complained to a priest that the idea that chastity must be practiced if a couple wished to avoid children was "asking too much" of the average person. The priest then asked the young man if he experienced any difficulty in abstaining whenever his employer sent him out of town. The man replied that indeed he practiced chastity during those times. It was easy to abstain from sex for business reasons, but "impossible" for moral ones!

As the other examples of voluntary abstention indicate, the requirement that a couple with good reasons for avoiding parenthood abstain for perhaps five days out of each month, is not so difficult to accomplish as many may believe. It is said to be even a custom among some people to abstain voluntarily for such periods because they are able to express a greater intensity of love and achieve greater mutual satisfaction after a fast. Just as a meal tastes better to a hungry man, so, too, does the act of sex have a greater appeal to those who have denied themselves for a short time.

Moreover, there seems to be substantial support from doctors for the opinion that most couples engage in intercourse to a much greater extent than they have a real need for, and that even if they reduced by half the number of times they performed the act, they would not appreciably increase sexual tension or frustration. Unfortunately, the world has so taken up the notion of sex as a medium of recreation that the typical man and wife think they should copulate whenever the slightest urge comes upon them. It has been said—truthfully—that a real *need* for sex is present in the act of the typical couple about as much as thirst is present in the alcoholic's need to drink.

HOW SELF-CONTROL IS DEVELOPED

Given the proper motivation—the realization that continence during a wife's fertile days is the only legitimate way by which a couple may avoid conception—is it usually possible for a couple to observe the necessary chastity? The answer would seem to be yes, at least for those who have learned to exercise restraint in their use of sex faculties. Nevertheless, it would be a mistake to think that conscious control over one's sexual impulses will not be necessary at various stages if the practice of chastity is to achieve its intended result. Such control is not developed overnight. Like a muscle in the body, it is strengthened by regular, systematic exercise.

Of great importance in developing self-control is the realization that the sex impulse thrives on stimulation. If left to itself, and undisturbed by outside influences, it can remain quiescent for long periods—periods much longer than most persons would imagine. This fact may be difficult for moderns to grasp, simply because their sex impulses are constantly being exploited by motion pictures, television programs, books, magazines. The purveyors of everything from soap to breakfast foods have concluded that if they titillate the senses and cause the public's mind to dwell on sex, they will sell more of their product. But even notwithstanding that our society constantly exploits our sex instincts for commercial gain, the fact remains that the average man and woman can easily overcome this stimulation and turn his or her mind to other things for long periods of time. It is possible even for young men to go many weeks without feeling any sexual urge when their minds are occupied by important matters.

It is no overstatement to say that, strong as is the sexual drive, it loses most of its power when it is brought under the domination of the mind. For proof that this is so, consider the case of the "frigid male" or "frigid female." In most cases, these men and women who cannot bring themselves to engage actively in the act of sex are examined by physicians who testify that they have nothing organically wrong. What they need is to have their minds turn on the traffic light which tells their bodies to proceed. But for many different reasons, perhaps stemming from childhood experiences or false ideas about the "dirtiness" of sex, they cannot do so. Their sexual appetites, therefore, are under complete domination of their minds and emotions.

On the other hand, consider the sexual pervert, the man who seems unable to exercise control over his appetite, or the woman who is promiscuous with every man she meets. When they are examined, physicians cannot find that they have any greater sexual drive than the average man or woman. What they have, however, is an attitude of mind which makes it difficult or impossible for them to restrain themselves. They have no physical need for their sexual excesses, but rather some mental or emotional need which they seek to express in this way.

Further evidence of the part that the mind plays in creating or braking the sexual impulse is the fact that what arouses one person will repel another. Hardly any "stimulus" can be said to arouse equally all men and women. It is only what the individual mind chooses to make of it. True, most people in a given culture may react in a certain way to what they see or hear. For instance, a strip-tease dancer goes through a routine which inflames the passions of perhaps most of her male audience. But this is a result of the conditioning they have received. In another time and place, her display might provoke only boredom and indifference.

In Western countries, a young woman with uncovered breasts may arouse sexual desires. A native in deep Africa sees such a sight every day, there is nothing remarkable about it, and he observes it with indifference. On the other hand, he regards a fat woman as highly desirable sexually. Confront him with a thin white woman—the Western "ideal"—and he would find her repulsive.

In fact, the sexual attraction which a husband and wife feel for each other is largely a result of habit controlled by the will. Husbands and wives have often commented that they disliked each other the first time they met or were indifferent to each other. In some cases, men and women knew each other for years, never experiencing any sense of sexual magnetism, before they began dating. It is obvious that if they had chosen not to see each other, never to date, and never to marry, that they would not feel the sexual desire for each other that they do.

The point of all this is that, to a greater extent than most people realize, their sexual desires are operated from the control point of their minds. Instead of an act that is performed instinctually such as an animal might perform it, the human act of sex can be put under the will. It is of

vital importance that men and women understand that
their instincts should not dictate when they should have
sexual relations, but that they were made to dominate the
instinct. When we talk about self-control, therefore, we
talk not about mastery of the organ but mastery of the
whole man.

Of course, if the will had no power to control one's sexual activities, the marriage ceremony itself would be a
meaningless farce. In receiving this sacrament, the bridegroom and bride promise to love each other until death.
The very fact that they make this promise implies that
they have the power to keep it. It means that they have
the power to be faithful to each other. Even if one partner
should become ill or unable to perform the sexual act
even for many years, the other promises to remain faithful. This means that he or she has the power to resist
temptations to be unfaithful.

In fact, in this power to be chaste man separates himself from the lower animals. An animal performs the act
of reproduction simply as a result of an instinctual drive.
It cannot exercise a conscious choice when to perform the
act, nor even to choose the partner with which to perform
it. Unless man exercises a conscious, deliberate control
over his sexual desires, he differs in no way in this respect
from an animal.

Of course, if man lacked the power to do this and were
merely a tool of his passions, it would be absurd to speak
of sin and absurd to hold him responsible for the deeds he
has committed. It is this view that man has no control
over himself that many secularists seem to hold.

They seem to believe that man is a creature of instincts;
that when passion calls, man must answer. When their

beliefs are held up to light, it can be seen that they espouse the kind of sexual freedom that animals have been enjoying since the beginning of time.

Development of control over sex requires much practice. It is not something that comes suddenly—something that a husband or wife will suddenly have when its need arises. Rather, it is built upon little things—the daily habit of saying "no" to one's self, when to say "yes" would work against the best interests of one's partner. Great successes will be built, little by little, upon the smaller. In the practice of chastity, as in most other things, nothing succeeds like success.

As an everyday matter, the control of the sex appetite by the mind means that the individual must control the reactions to things he or she sees or hears or which enter the consciousness in other ways. A desire for sexual relations usually does not come upon an individual with a rush. Generally it has small beginnings. These can be curbed when they are first experienced, or they can be left unmolested or even encouraged until the desire becomes greater and more difficult to manage.

The advice, "Know thyself," never has a more pertinent meaning than it does regarding an individual's responses to certain stimulations. You must understand how, as a result of your training and conditioning, you react to certain stimuli. Knowing this, you must then put your will into combat with your reflexes which may have been conditioned over a long period of time.

THE POWER OF CONFIDENCE

Only an optimist or fool would contend that chastity is always easy. To "put your body at the service of your will, and your will at the service of God" requires not only great self-discipline and self-knowledge—but also the ability and determination to acquire these priceless ingredients. As Pope Pius XI wrote in his encyclical on Christian marriage:

"Even the very best instruction given by the Church will not alone suffice to re-create conformity of marriage to the law of God; something more is needed in addition to the education of the mind, namely, a steadfast determination of the will, on the part of husband and wife, to observe the sacred laws of God and of nature in regard to marriage."

The married man and woman who succeed in practicing chastity first believe that it is possible to do so. As in the performance of most things, the person with confidence has half the battle won. A revealing story to this effect is told about an incident involving the Admirals David Glasgow Farragut and Samuel Francis Du Pont during the American Civil War. Admiral Farragut called Du Pont before him to explain why the latter had failed to penetrate Charleston harbor, as he had been instructed to do. Du Pont gave an elaborate list of reasons. After listening patiently, Farragut said: "And there is another reason why you failed. You didn't believe you could succeed." Farragut himself proved the power of self-confidence when, against heavy odds, he forced his way into the bay at Mobile, destroyed many enemy ships and captured the forts. It was here that he gave birth to his memorable slogan, "Damn the torpedoes! Go ahead!"

GOD'S PLAN FOR SEX IN MARRIAGE

This, then, is the place of sex in marriage:

God created it to serve as a means of procreation. But it is a means by which a husband and wife may demonstrate mutual affection. When properly used, it also serves as a source of love.

A husband and wife may engage in intercourse as long as they do not deliberately attempt to prevent the act from reaching its natural conclusion. If they engage in sex, they must be willing to accept the responsibility of parenthood if that should be the natural result. But they should not feel that there is anything wrong in their enjoyment of this act, even though conception does not result from it.

Sex is a means of expressing love and also of strengthening love. But it is not love of itself. True love—a sense of selflessness, consideration, and concern for the welfare of one's partner—can thrive without sex. In fact, the willingness to forego the marital act for worthy motives can be a higher form of love than participation in the marital act itself.

Every couple must practice chastity, by which is meant that they must use their sex faculties according to right reason. Chastity is an essential element for the success of any marriage. A loving relationship cannot exist without it, for there are times in every marriage when one person must consider the welfare of the other and must be willing to abstain from intercourse.

Doing without the sexual act when the times require is not difficult if a person has a strong desire to do so. The average married person engages in the sexual act to a greater extent than is necessary to appease his basic sex appetite. Just as most persons eat more food than they absolutely need to appease hunger if given the opportunity, so, too, do most husbands and wives have coitus more than is necessary to release their tensions. This use of sex above and beyond what might be considered necessary is not wrong in itself. But it indicates that there is a large "margin for sacrifice" which men and women can use without hardship when the occasion requires.

Some men and women have higher native intelligence than others. Some have personality characteristics which are more likely to enable them to lead holy lives. Some have more earthly goods than others. So, too, have some men and women a need to practice abstinence to a greater extent than others. In some marriages, this abstinence may be necessary because one of the partners is chronically ill. In another, because the husband must spend long periods away from home. In a third, because a couple for one reason or other should not have a child.

Now let us move on to consider the proper and practical reasons justifying family limitation.

7.

Justification for
a Small Family

As we have seen, the procreation and education of children is the positive work of marriage. And the large family is the Christian ideal—the one which, in the words of Pope Pius XII, is "blessed by God, beloved by the Church, and considered by it as one of its most precious treasures."

But the Church recognizes that there are sound reasons for the sane regulation of births. She does not want Christians to bring children into the world without regard to consequences, whether they be spiritual, emotional, physical, economic, or social. In order to uphold the basic dignity of man as a creature of God, every family is entitled to these reasonable expectations:

1. Every family has the right to strive for the economic necessities of life, as well as comforts considered "ordinary" in its environment. For instance, in highly prosperous regions such as the United States, Canada, and the countries of Western Europe, a couple would not have

unreasonable aspirations if they sought to have meat on the table once a day, while in undeveloped parts of the world, the couple that can afford meat daily is an exception.

Similarly, a couple might reasonably expect to be on a sound economic footing before undertaking the expense of a new child. They are entitled to avoid being plunged into debt to cover doctors' and hospital bills that they could not pay off within a reasonable period. It is reasonable, too, for them to want to provide their children with at least as much education as might be considered average for their environment and as much as they will need to lead a decent life in the years ahead.

To state this in another way, a husband and wife have a right to aspire to living standards for their children at least equal to the standards they themselves knew in their younger years.

2. A husband and wife are entitled to avoid pregnancy if there is a serious probability that the health of the mother, father, existing children, or the unborn child would be seriously endangered as a result of having the child or providing for him. Of course, some physical inconveniences always attach to pregnancy. Generally, these are transient and leave no permanent ill effects. If a competent doctor believes serious damage could be done to any member of the family, however, a couple need not fulfill the obligation of parenthood. In fact, they might have a moral obligation under some circumstances to avoid having a baby.

3. Every child is entitled to the consistent care of both mother and father. A traveling salesman whose profession requires him to be away from home even two or three

weeks out of each month probably would be able to give his children the fatherly direction they need. On the other hand, a man whose job requires him to remain in a distant country for several years, where it would be inadvisable to have his family with him, probably would be unable to provide the necessary care and direction. In considering this principle, it is important to remember that a child's education is his parents' responsibility just as is his procreation, and that if circumstances beyond their control would render them unable to perform their teaching function in a fairly regular, consistent way, they might well consider whether they would be acting wisely if they procreated a child.

4. A couple are fully entitled to strive to have children without serious mental or physical defects. For example, prudence would strongly urge that they avoid having a baby if there is a strong possibility that the infant will be mentally retarded.

EXAMPLES OF PERSONS WHO MIGHT
PRACTICE PERIODIC CONTINENCE

How do these four principles work out in practice? Let us consider some typical examples.

• A mother had just given birth to her first child. While not a dangerous pregnancy, it caused much discomfort. She had nausea and morning sickness during the early stages, and a tendency towards diabetes in the latter ones. Normally weaker than average, as well as being emotionally high strung, she is not at all sure that she will be able to give her child all the care that will be necessary.

Her family's income is low and she will have to do all of the housework and care for the baby herself. For several months she will have to arise early in the morning and also in the middle of the night to feed her child. Her doctor has advised her against another pregnancy, at least until the first child is past infancy and will not require around-the-clock attention. Under such circumstances, the wife and husband could quite reasonably avoid having a second child until conditions become more favorable for the pregnancy.

• A woman with two small children has had four other pregnancies which were terminated by miscarriage. She has consulted the most respected obstetrician in her community, and he has told her that the only way she could hope to have another child would be by going to bed as soon as she thought she was pregnant and remaining there for almost the entire nine months. To do this, however, she would have to hire expensive help to do the housekeeping and take care of her existing children. But this would mean that she and her husband would have to go deeply into debt to pay for it. Under these circumstances, she would be justified in avoiding conception for as long a period as necessary.

• A husband has had an operation for cancer. The surgeon is optimistic, but will not say that the cancer will not recur, or that the husband can reasonably expect to live long enough to provide for the education of a new child. This situation would justify practicing periodic continence until the doctor could give more positive assurance that the husband would be able to fulfill his obligations as a father.

• A family with three children lives in a tense, wrought-up atmosphere. While other mothers let their youngsters play out of doors without supervision and to walk to school without fearing that they will be injured while crossing the street, this mother thinks it necessary to accompany them to school, feels that she must be on hand while they play out of doors so that she can "keep them from hurting themselves," and expresses her concern in many other ways. A perfectionist by nature, she spends many hours doing things for them that most mothers do not think they should do.

Although this mother is overcautious and is mistaken in her fears, the fact remains that she could not easily have a fourth child without enduring mental anguish during her pregnancy not only over the welfare of the existing three but over her ability to do all the work required by a fourth child as well. Considering this woman's state of mind, and the possibility that her health would be harmed by her own attitudes, it would seem licit for her and her husband to observe periodic continence until she had the time she would need to care for a fourth child.

Meanwhile, however, she might be well advised to seek professional guidance. A psychologist, psychiatrist, family doctor, or pediatrician in whom she has confidence, might help her develop more easygoing attitudes which would enable her to carry the responsibilities of motherhood with less stress and strain.

• The only child of a young husband and wife has contracted a serious disease which could lead to her permanent crippling unless specified medical treatments are carried out by the mother under the doctor's instructions. This will mean that the mother must devote three or four hours every day to caring for the child for several years in order to insure complete recovery. If she becomes pregnant, she will be unable to give this much time to the child.

• A husband or wife have a strain of insanity running through the family. While we do not have positive answers to all the questions concerning the characteristics transmitted from one generation to another, it is generally agreed that some types of insanity can be inherited. In situations of this kind, the best available medical or scientific advice should be followed. A competent medical man told this couple that a serious defect would probably be transmitted from the parents to child. The husband and wife therefore are justified in seeking to avoid parenthood.

• A woman has been under the treatment of a psychiatrist for a nervous condition. He believes that her condition might worsen if she became pregnant, and that in any event she now could not give a child the loving care and acceptance everyone needs to become an emotionally mature adult. Here, naturally, is ample reason for family limitation.

The whole question of eugenics is very complicated and even experts often disagree about traits which can—or cannot—be inherited. Moreover, parents who themselves suffer defects may be capable of producing normal children, while intelligent and emotionally stable parents may have children who are mentally deficient. Notwithstanding the fact that much remains to be learned about the genes and chromosomes which are transmitted from generation to generation, a couple will be acting morally if they accept the best evidence available when they must decide whether to have another child.

• A family already has several children, and the husband and wife face a constant struggle to meet the monthly payments for rent, food, clothing, and other necessities. The husband holds a fairly secure position but it offers no reason to hope that his income will rise substantially in the near future. If this couple have another child, they believe that children then existing would have to be cared for by a neighbor while the wife took a job to augment the family's income. Obviously, the coming of a child would cause severe economic hardship and perhaps even cause the existing children to be denied the regular, continuous care of their mother. The resort to periodic continence would be a lesser evil.

• A husband holds a job which gives him free time to continue his education but does not pay enough to support a child. In a few years, as a result of the training he is undertaking, he probably will be able to support a family. If he now took another job paying a salary that would enable him to support children, he would have to discontinue his education, and drop his plans for advancement. During this temporary period, during which he is preparing to fulfill his responsibilities as a husband and father, he would probably have a legitimate reason to use periodic continence.

• A family including three children live in a crowded city apartment. Two boys and one girl share one bedroom and will need an additional bedroom as they grow older. For almost a year, the parents have been searching for a new place to live, but every suitable apartment at a price they could afford has been designated "for adults only." Landlords who learn that they have three children and are of childbearing age show an immediate disinclination to rent. The couple lack sufficient savings for a home of their own, and to a considerable extent, therefore, they are at the mercy of the apartment-house owners.

If they had a fourth child, they would probably have to move to larger quarters which could be found only in a run-down section where they believe their children would be exposed to bad influences.

Such a couple could not be criticized for their decision to resort to periodic continence. Any sin that might be involved in the account above would certainly rest more upon the landlords who refuse to endanger their profits by renting to large families, and perhaps also upon the civic officials and other leaders of society who fail to provide adequate living quarters for parents with children.

As all of the foregoing examples suggest, situations in which periodic continence may be used legitimately are varied and comprehensive. These examples fall within the boundaries for the legitimate regulation of births that were outlined by Pope Pius XII, in 1951, in an address to the Catholic Union of Midwives of Italy. At that time, the Holy Father declared that under certain conditions a couple need not fulfill the "positive work" of parenthood. He stated:

"Marriage binds to a state of life which, while conferring certain rights, at the same time imposes the accomplishment of a positive work which belongs to the very state of wedlock. This being so, the general principle can now be stated that the fulfillment of a positive duty may

be withheld should grave reasons, independent of the good will of those obliged to it, show that such fulfillment is untimely, or make it evident that it cannot equitably be demanded.

"Serious reasons, often put forward on medical, eugenic, economic, and social grounds, can exempt from the obligatory service for a considerable period of time, even for the entire duration of the marriage. It follows from this that the use of the infertile periods can be lawful from the moral point of view and, in the circumstances which have been mentioned, it is indeed lawful. If, however, in the light of a reasonable and fair judgment, there are no such serious personal reasons, or reasons deriving from external circumstances, then the habitual intention to avoid the fruitfulness of the union, while at the same time continuing fully to satisfy sensual intent, can only arise from a false appreciation of life and from motives that run counter to true standards of moral conduct."

It is interesting to note that the "horrible examples of parenthood" generally cited by the contraceptionists are covered by the Pope's statement. Thus, the woman whose health might be seriously endangered if she undertook another pregnancy would be justified in avoiding such a pregnancy. The couple with a large family in a tiny home, and without reasonable prospects of finding larger quarters, would be dispensed from the obligation of further parenthood. Then there is the typical case often cited to "prove" the Church's "inhumane attitude": A husband and wife are already parents of six children or so. They live in a shabby home, often lack enough food to eat, go without needed medical care, lack warm clothing in winter. In addition, the children receive no example of good conduct from their father or mother. Should such a couple have more children? If they do, it is for reasons other than their religion.

⌐ To repeat: Whenever a genuine reason exists, a couple may be dispensed from the obligation of parenthood. However, we must not confuse legitimate reasons for avoiding conception with convenient reasons. For example, there is a sharp distinction between an uncomfortable pregnancy and a dangerous one. Many women suffer from nausea during the early stages of pregnancy. There may be discomfort resulting from heartburn during the latter stages, some difficulty and discomfort with backache, leg cramps, and abdominal cramps, perhaps an inability to sleep. These conditions might be called "normal" in pregnancy, although some women go through the entire nine-month period without any discomfort.

In fact, cases in which a mother would seriously endanger her health by becoming pregnant are much rarer than most people believe. Dr. Robert J. Walsh, assistant attending obstetrician and gynecologist at St. Vincent's Hospital, New York, and Fellow of the American College of Obstetrics and Gynecology, states that few obstetricians have ever seen a case in which they could say with certainty that a mother would die if she carried a child until it could be born alive.

Writing in the *Catholic Guide to Expectant Motherhood*, Dr. Walsh states:

"There are some conditions—severe heart disease, hypertension, nephritis, etc.—where it may be more dangerous for a woman to have a child than it would be normally. But the mortality rate from childbirth, even for women with the most serious conditions, is almost negligible to-

day. Even a woman in extremely poor physical condition has an excellent chance of survival.

"One Catholic hospital in New York takes many of these
most difficult obstetrical cases to be found, including patients who have left other doctors who suggested therapeutic abortions. Of some six thousand cases, it has had
but one fatality."

WHY A SIMPLE FORMULA IS IMPOSSIBLE

The question would be greatly simplified, of course,
if we could devise a formula exactly stating who could
and could not use periodic continence legitimately. Sometimes a husband and wife will indicate disappointment
because such a formula does not exist. They would like
to have it said, for instance, that a couple with an income
of $100 a week can afford one child; when their income
advances to $125, they can provide for a second child;
and with each additional twenty-five dollars or thirty dollars increase in weekly income, another infant can be conceived. Such a formula would simplify discussion and
provide a handy guide for everyone. But it is completely
impractical in fact. The truth is that each case must be
decided upon the particular circumstances which apply
to it. Unless one knows all the factors that affect an individual couple, it is impossible to say with certainty
whether they have valid reasons for avoiding conception. One can never say offhand that the couple with one
or two children—or with no children—is justified or not in
avoiding pregnancy. Too many intimate details—often
known only to the husband and wife, and so private that

they would not disclose them to anyone but a confessor—
are involved.

For example, consider the case of a husband and wife
in their late twenties. They now have three children. Both
the man and woman come from a family with upper-
class background. Ever since infancy, they have known
the ordinary luxuries of life—a family automobile, attractive home in a middle-class community, clothing more
expensive than the average. Their parents provided them
with an education in moderately expensive colleges and
gave them a taste for the so-called "good things of life."

The husband now works as a bank clerk—a position
which imposes certain expensive obligations upon him. He
is expected to appear for work carefully groomed. As a representative of the bank, he is expected to live in a certain
type of home—not the most expensive in the community,
but nevertheless more expensive than the average. If he
wishes to be considered for a better position, he and his
wife are also expected to attend various social functions
in the community. This means that she must have a higher
allowance for personal grooming than would be necessary
for most women with such an income. And when they
attend such social functions, they must hire a baby sitter
to care for their children.

In spite of these expenses which are, in effect, a necessary part of his job, the husband earns a discouragingly
modest salary. In fact, an acquaintance who left school at
the age of sixteen and is an attendant in a gasoline station,
takes home a larger income than the college-educated
bank employee. Given these circumstances, the husband
and his wife have searched their souls and have concluded that—for the present—they cannot afford a fourth

child and continue to maintain the position expected of them.

Are they justified in their conclusion? Possibly. The husband here balances his prospects for advancement in his chosen profession and the consequences of having another child at this time. His wife should not be obliged to become a wage earner in order to support a new life. In other words, there are imponderables involved in every such decision and while others might act differently, in the last analysis, this particular husband and wife have made an honest decision with clear conscience and without base selfishness.

Next, consider the case of the gas-station attendant mentioned above. He was a member of a happy-go-lucky family, one without high social aspirations and content with the simple pleasures of family life. His father had worked all his life with his hands, was content with an inexpensive home, and never owned more than one suit of clothing at any time in his life.

The son was brought up with this set of values. He could see no need for formal schooling beyond the years the law required, and eagerly took a job where he could be around automobiles. A few years later he was in a position to marry and begin raising a family. His own parents had never regarded their six children as a burden, but always had felt that they had been blessed by God. He looked forward to parenthood with the same spirit. The girl he married—from the same background and with the same aspirations as himself—also wanted a large family. Now they have four children and await a fifth as soon as God sees fit to give them another.

They will be unable to provide many luxuries for their

new child, and would clothe it mostly with garments that already have been handed down from one child to the other. Nor would they have a housing crisis if another baby came. They themselves were accustomed to sharing bedrooms with brothers or sisters; in fact, they think it is better for a child to share a room rather than to spend too much time alone. Nor are they sure that they will be able to pay any child's way to college. But they do not think it damages a youngster if he must work to pay some of his own expenses. They believe, as did Peter Finley Dunne, the turn-of-the-century humorist, speaking through his character, Mr. Dooley: "I don't think it makes anny difference wan way or th' other how free ye make an idjacation. Men that wants it'll have it be hook an' be crook, an' thim that don't re-aly want it niver will get it. Ye can lade a man up to th' university, but ye can't make him think."

A person who does not understand all the factors in the problem of the bank employee and his wife might say that they were shirking their responsibility by limiting their family to three children. Another person might consider it "disgraceful" that the gasoline-station attendant and his wife should have so many children, when they line up before a solitary bathroom in their house, use a car that is eight years old, and sometimes appear in public with patches on their clothing. Both conclusions would be wrong: They fail to consider the backgrounds, training, and aspirations of the parents involved.

These examples indicate why we cannot devise a clear-cut formula that answers all the questions a couple may ask. In every case, a rule of reason must prevail. But this rule is not difficult to observe. When men and women take time to consider their circumstances carefully, they usually reach an honest conclusion as to whether to have more children. It is possible, of course, that they will mistake their capacity to care for another child. In the light of the fact that God's providence should not be underestimated, it would be well for such couples—if they must err at all—to err on the side of generosity even if their decision might cause some minor hardship.

COUPLES MUST DECIDE FOR THEMSELVES

From all that we have considered before, it is obvious that the children born to any couple should be the result of *thoughtful* and *deliberate* choice.

In determining family size, a husband and wife face a variety of choices. Only their consciences and their characters move them in one direction or another. They may elect to exercise their marital prerogatives frequently, occasionally, rarely, or not at all. When they do, they may positively will to have a child or another child, if that also be God's will, or they may have the willingness to accept whatever God sends them as a result of their use of marriage.

In either case, they are making a deliberate choice. Granted the purity of their motives and the prudence of their circumstances, the children which result—if they be a dozen or only two—are the result of virtuous living.

In making decisions about the procreation and education of children, it is the right intention which distinguishes the Christian couple from the pagan. As Pope

Pius XII said, "In this matter, everything depends on the intention."

What should Christian married people intend about family size when they enter marriage?

They must recognize that marriage is more God's property than theirs—as the priesthood is, of course.

They must love the idea of having children or at least be willing to accept childbearing and child-raising as the basic work of marriage.

They must be generous in their approach to parenthood and work toward more than a mere minimum accomplishment.

They must be optimists, knowing that God works with them, that He has reasons and plans for them which will be revealed perhaps as they grow old, perhaps only in eternity.

They must work together without injury to the rights of their spouse.

They must never, with God's help, defile their marriage bed by sinful acts, either solitary, mutual, or social (e.g. adultery).

They must work together intelligently, using their gifts of reason to do what is best and right for each other, respecting each other's attitudes and shortcomings, as well as the physical, social, and spiritual needs of their children.

Most Christian couples have these right intentions. Granting all of the weaknesses of human flesh, the pressures of secular life, and occasional lapses of one form or another, most Christians strive for these ideals and, by the end of their lives, succeed in realizing more of them than the world will admit.

A discussion of reasons that enable a couple to postpone parenthood would be incomplete without reaffirmation of the fact that the child received with open arms and given the love of his parents and other members of the family is truly entering the environment most likely to help him become a God-fearing, stable citizen.

The Church does not shut her eyes to the fact that it is extremely costly in time, money, and effort to bring children into the world, to feed and educate them and to keep them healthy in soul, mind, and body. But with her wisdom based upon experience through the centuries, she also knows that a family does not need material riches—a shiny new car, spotless furniture, expensive cuts of meat for every dinner, or the care of a medical specialist for every illness, in order to thrive and be happy. In fact, couples who have these material possessions but lack a high motive for living which only an unswerving belief in God can provide, are indeed the most miserable of beings. One need only witness the parade of the wealthy but miserable to the psychiatrists' couches to be convinced of the truth of this statement.

It is with the consideration that a child is a blessing from God who will bring joy and light to his parents that a couple should decide whether they can reasonably have another baby. A husband and wife should try to reach their conclusion in the light of the fact that their marriage offers the opportunity to participate in one of the greatest of human acts—the creation of a human being in God's image and likeness, with the opportunity of helping the child to take his place in Heaven at the end of his days. When husbands and wives appreciate the opportunity which God offers them, and when they realize that the things of the spirit which they can give their child are of greater importance to his welfare than material luxuries, they will have a good attitude upon which to base their decision.

With such an attitude, if they must conclude that they cannot prudently have another child, they will make their decision with a sense of sadness. For the Christian couple, the decision to limit births will not be a happy way to get out from under responsibility, but a necessary step taken with the knowledge that it is depriving them of a great opportunity to serve in partnership with God in one of the most important works possible.

A husband and wife who are considering whether to have a baby at this time need not consult a priest to help them make up their minds. It is true that their pastor may provide them with some viewpoints they have overlooked. Similar help may be provided by an older couple who may have had problems like those which the younger husband and wife now face. In the last analysis, of course, the decision must be made by the couple alone and it should satisfy their own good consciences.

The nature of their decision requires that they make it together and in a spirit of mutual love and consideration. This is a requisite whether they decide to have a child or not. If they decide in favor of having a baby, each should understand the responsibilities involved for both self and spouse. If they decide not to conceive, they should understand that they will have to abstain from intercourse whenever it may result in pregnancy. For the regulation of births involves the regulation of intercourse.

Because of their love for each other, this dual regulation should result from a mutual decision. Neither should want to make a solo decision that would cause serious emotional or physical hardship to the other or lead to sins outside the marriage relationship. In fact, the marriage contract to which husband and wife agree on their wedding day specifies that neither can decide to deprive the other of marital rights without a truly serious reason.

When conditions exist that would excuse a couple from having children, either for a short period or for the duration of their marriage, it must be remembered that the only moral way that they can avoid conception is by abstaining from intercourse when the wife is fertile. When the couple abstain, they do nothing to obstruct the natural law. They impose no artificial means to prevent the act of sex from following its natural conclusion. Hence commit no sin.

BOTH HUSBAND AND WIFE MUST AGREE

The necessity of abstinence when there is a sufficient reason for avoiding conception means that, in justice, two additional requirements must be met:

1. Both husband and wife must be willing to use this method of family limitation.

2. In doing so, both must be able to avoid sin.

Let us examine these conditions more closely. Why must both husband and wife agree on the practice of periodic abstinence? Because, in a very real sense, use of this method involves a changing of the conditions under which the husband and wife agreed to marry. When the marriage contract was made, the wife agreed to give herself to her husband in marital relations whenever he reasonably asked her to do so. Barring serious illness, etc., a wife must be willing to engage in intercourse with her husband when he so requests. A husband has the same obligation to satisfy reasonable requests by his wife.

The fact that both love and the marriage contract require one marriage partner to engage in sexual relations when the other reasonably and seriously requests it means that neither, by himself or herself alone, can decide to practice abstinence. Periodic continence is therefore practicable and lawful only when both partners agree to it. It cannot justly be practiced if either partner wishes to discontinue it.

Serious difficulties on this score are unlikely, however, if a serious reason exists for avoiding pregnancy and both partners have a deep and loving concern for the other's welfare. Assume that the carrying of a child would affect a wife's health. It is unlikely that a loving husband would refuse to observe periodic continence. Or assume that the financial burden of supporting another child would be more than the husband could bear. A loving wife would understand this—and co-operate with him. In practice, therefore, when a husband and wife live in an atmosphere of mutual love and respect, their decision to abstain on the fertile days will be made with the full consent of both of them. Their marriage would lack the basic necessities of love if one person deliberately chose to abstain from sexual relations over the objections of the other.

A difference of opinion is more likely to arise later, when for one reason or another, one wishes to discontinue the practice. The desire to stop using the method may be due to a genuine desire for a child, or may result from the unwillingness or inability of one partner to abstain for the required time. Just as both parties must agree in order to begin this method, so, too, must both agree in order to continue it. If one person wishes to stop, the other is morally obliged to do so. Again, the reason derives from considerations of both love and the marriage contract, for the wife should wish intercourse whenever her husband reasonably requests it, and the husband should also accede lovingly to his wife's request.

The reason for the requirement that both parties must be able to avoid sin also is easy to understand. Periodic continence must not be practiced under circumstances which might serve as occasions of other sins. If a husband and wife forego intercourse, they must be able to control themselves so that they do not seek to satisfy their sexual appetites in other ways.

This requirement may be a stumbling block for men and women who do not fully accept the necessity for chastity in marriage as well as in the single life. It will also be difficult for the man or woman who believes that the sexual appetite must be appeased as soon as it appears. It will also be difficult for the man or woman who does not wholeheartedly accept periodic abstinence as the only legitimate way of avoiding contraception.

Sins to which this method might lead fall into several categories. The couple themselves might sin against the Sixth Commandment by engaging in all of the preliminaries of coitus and achieving an orgasm without having actual intercourse. In doing this, the couple would be actually practicing a prohibited form of contraception. Any deliberate orgasm by either or both parties which thwarts the deposit of the husband's seed in his wife's vagina is a violation of the Sixth Commandment.

Another common danger is that the husband or wife will practice masturbation—reaching sexual satisfaction with or without the co-operation of the other.

A third danger—and perhaps the greatest of all—is that the husband or wife will seek sexual satisfaction outside of marriage. This is a particular hazard for men, but it is by no means an unknown danger for women, particularly when wives move about freely outside their homes.

These dangers that the practice of periodic continence may lead to sins of impurity can be largely overcome if the couple have an idealistic motivation. If they are prepared to make the momentary sacrifice gladly in order to perfect their own spiritual welfare and that of their children, they will have the basis upon which to resist temptations.

From the foregoing discussion, we may summarize briefly the circumstances under which a couple would be justified in avoiding the birth of a first child, spacing their family as their particular needs suggest, or deciding not to have additional children. These circumstances are:

1. They have a good reason. As we have seen, this reason may be economic, medical (including physical and emotional), social, or eugenic.

2. Both concur in the decision. Because of their love for each other—and their marriage contract itself—neither would want to deprive the other of the marital act without his or her approval.

3. When necessary, they are able to abstain from intercourse without serious difficulty.

COMMON QUESTIONS ABOUT FAMILY
REGULATION

When conditions under which couples may practice periodic continence are discussed, the following questions sometimes arise:

How many children should a couple have? This is a decision which they must make, and for which they must accept responsibility. Of course, the Church likes large families, and her attitude is the result not of sentiment, but of religious conviction. On January 20, 1958, for example, Pope Pius XII made this observation: "Whenever you find large families in great numbers, they point to the physical and moral health of a Christian people; a living faith in God and trust in His Providence; the fruitful and joyful holiness of Catholic marriage." He went on to make the "large" family and the "Christian" family virtually synonymous. What the Pope implied is that lots of children are good for the married couple, for the children themselves, for society, and that society is sick when it looks upon fruitfulness in marriage as "a social malady."

But note that the Holy Father spoke of society in general, of people in general. He did not speak of Mr. and Mrs. John Jones on East Main Street.

It is also important to realize what he, and the Church, are *not* talking about.

When we speak of the large family, we do not specify any particular number. Four or five children might constitute a large family in metropolitan New York, yet the "average" in rural Argentina.

Nor do we relegate to the outer regions of Hades those relatively sterile couples whom Providence decrees to be the parents of few or no children.

Is it permissible to use periodic continence at the beginning of marriage? In general, a couple should not marry unless they are prepared to do the primary work of marriage—the procreation and education of children. But as we have seen, marriage serves other purposes as well. It is a means by which one spouse may provide mutual aid and comfort to the other. It also is a way to relieve concupiscence, which means that if it is difficult or impossible for a single couple to avoid sins of impurity, they are better off married. As St. Paul said, "It is better to marry than to burn."

In modern society there may be many instances in which it may be desirable for newlyweds to defer parenthood. A typical example is that of the young man who completes his military service at age twenty-two or twenty-three and deems it necessary to resume his education. He is at an age when the desire for female companionship, love, and sexual satisfaction are strong. He believes it would be difficult to remain celibate for another three or four years. But, he would be unable to continue his education if he had to provide for a new family.

Under such circumstances, he and his wife would probably have a legitimate reason for deferring parenthood. The presumption is, of course, that they intend to fulfill their obligation to become parents later.

Even when a young couple might be justified in deferring parenthood, however, practical reasons argue against the extended practice of periodic continence early in marriage. The only opportunity for many people of low fertility to become parents exists in the early years of marriage, for fertility diminishes with age. Couples who begin marriage with a low potentiality may discover that by the time they try to have children, they are no longer able to do so.

Many studies have established that a woman's capacity for childbearing reaches its height in the late teens. It then drops off gradually until her thirties, when the decline becomes appreciably sharper. On the average, only one wife in seventeen is sterile—unable to have children —in her early twenties. But of wives in their late twenties, one in ten is sterile; and of those in their early thirties, one in six. A man's ability to become a father also wanes with age.

The point is self-evident. A young couple have no way of knowing whether they are fertile unless they have the actual experience of attempting conception, and those who wait too long before trying to conceive a child may discover that they no longer can do so.

Incidentally, this fact—that the older you are, the less likely your chances of becoming a parent—is useful knowledge for those persons who can foresee that they will be unable to support more than a few children. For the best safeguard against too many pregnancies is a late marriage. Much of the overpopulation problem of India results from the fact that the typical Indian bride is sixteen years of age or younger. If India could educate her young people to wait four or more years longer before they marry, many of her problems would be automatically taken care of.

It is also well to remember that we cannot foresee the future. Reasons which now seem highly compelling to avoid conception may prove later to have been unduly pessimistic.

For example, during the years just before the end of World War II, a young husband was working at a job which offered poor prospects for advancement, and he seemed doomed to a lifetime as a low wage earner. However, his firm enjoyed a spectacular postwar expansion, and he found himself being promoted rapidly. Within five years he was earning three times as much as he had earned before.

He and his wife had "played it safe," however, and had had only two children. Then one summer, when the youngsters were in their teens, they went boating on a lake. An accident occurred, the boat overturned, and one lad was unable to swim to shore. In trying to save his brother, the second boy also was dragged down. This sudden accident left the couple childless, and at an age when they could not have more children.

Another couple had only one child—a daughter. They felt that they could not afford other children, and from a strictly technical point of view, they were perhaps correct. However, it would by no means have been difficult for them to have had several additional children.

They had believed that they could count on her aid and comfort if they needed it in their old age. The daughter married a young engineer working for a large oil company. A few years after the marriage, the young husband was transferred to Venezuela and his wife naturally accompanied him. They have been gone eight years now, and the couple, who had hoped for a child to comfort their old age are now, in effect, childless.

Many similar examples prove that it is indeed impossible to foretell the future. True, it may bring unexpected hardship for the large family as well. A father of six children who has just buried his wife and now raises his children singlehandedly may momentarily question the wisdom of having had that number. But after watching his children develop a sense of responsibility toward the family as a whole and toward each individual member, he feels a great inspiration. Even though he faces a situation at which many outsiders shake their heads sadly, he can testify that human beings can do much more than they believe possible, and that a Christian motivated by sincere love of God and family can achieve miracles of sacrifice and accomplishment.

What can one person do if his or her spouse insists upon the use of contraceptives? When a disagreement over the practice of periodic continence unfortunately arises, it signifies that a deep problem exists, because it evidences a breakdown in the sense of co-operation which is the essence of harmonious marriage.

When this question arises, it indicates that one partner wishes to go in one direction while the other goes in another. It constitutes as severe a strain on the marriage as if the husband decided to move from New York to Africa and his wife was unwilling and unprepared to go.

Before a couple reach the point where they disagree on the question of contraception, their union probably has already deteriorated badly. For when they disagree on this, they disagree on a basic principle of marriage.

A partner who insists upon using conceptives against the other's wishes usually provokes one of three reactions: The innocent party (1) fights back; (2) complies and suffers in conscience; or (3) says in effect: "I'll submit to your demands in this area, but I'll wreak my revenge in other ones."

But a person convinced against his will remains unpersuaded still. If one spouse insists upon contraception, it is likely that the other's resentment will manifest itself in other ways. There will be fights over other matters. And that is why it is important that a man and woman discuss their plans and aspirations, and agree on the fundamental practices of marriage, before they even agree to marry.

As to the moral considerations:

No Catholic in right conscience can willingly co-operate in sin. He or she must make the offending party understand that he or she repudiates contraception. If the mind of the innocent person is stated clearly and the other continues to insist, the innocent one may passively submit if it is necessary to avoid the breakup of the marriage, protect the welfare of the children, or avoid other grave consequences. He or she may have to suffer in silence, remembering the words of Christ, "If any man will come after me, let him deny himself, and take up his cross, and follow me." (Matthew, 16:24.)

If this problem arises, it might be well for both parties to discuss their differences with a third party or to consider alternatives to contraceptives. Perhaps the solution lies in seeing a good doctor for instructions in the proper use of periodic continence.

The situation is different if the partner favoring contraceptives insists that the other use them. The second must refuse. He or she may never be an active co-operator in evil.

Is the danger of "overpopulation" of the human race a legitimate reason? This question, frequently asked in the

United States, Canada, Western Europe, and Australia, results from the widespread campaign of propaganda waged with respect to the peoples of Asia and Latin America principally. In North America and Europe, there is little danger of a "population explosion" which would deny the average child the expectation of adequate food, clothing, shelter, and educational opportunity. In fact, living standards in these countries have risen to heights that past generations never dreamed of. The actual problem they face is not how to find sufficient food, but rather how to dispose of the surplus crops which farm machines and the widespread use of fertilizers and scientific-planting methods have made possible. For most persons in those areas, the threat of "overpopulation" is not immediate, and it is unlikely that any person living there could legitimately use such a reason for limiting the size of his family. It is possible that overcrowded living conditions in certain small areas may make it difficult for a family to house their children adequately, and they would therefore be justified in avoiding conception. But this would be a strictly local situation.

In Latin America and many Asiatic countries—for example, India and Ceylon—the overpopulation problem is a very real one. True, the problem in its basic form is not that too many people are living in those areas but rather that man has failed to make use of the resources which God has given him. Nevertheless, many children born in those areas will either suffer severe hunger or, if their parents are prosperous, they will consume food, clothing, and other necessities and thereby force some other child to do without.

Theologians have reached different conclusions regarding the justfication of periodic continence under such circumstances. Father Anthony F. Zimmerman believes that "the family has no duty to restrict the number of children in order to avoid overpopulation." Other theologians maintain that man has a duty to procreate only as long as the population of the world is not sufficiently provided for, and thereafter an obligation to have a large family in overpopulated areas is not binding upon the individual.

Says John R. Connery, S.J.: "Scholastic theologians maintained that the duty to procreate was incumbent on everyone immediately after the Fall and until such time as the population of the world was sufficiently provided for. After that it became a common obligation and no longer bound the individual. The individual would then be free to marry or not to marry. Pius XII defined the obligation more precisely in his talk to Italian midwives when he stated that it fell on married couples who made use of the marriage right, but again he related the obligation to population needs. It should follow from all this that as population needs change one could expect the duty to procreate to adjust accordingly." This general opinion is also held by John Ford, S.J., Joseph Duhamel, S.J., Gerald Kelly, S.J., and other participants in the 1959 meeting of the Catholic Theological Society.

In the view of this writer there is little doubt that an individual couple might properly limit their family size out of consideration for the general well-being of their country and that a particular national government might recommend prudence in childbearing to young families. We presume, of course, that no pressure is used to limit the family's right to be a family, and that no immoral means of family limitation are suggested.

Would a couple be wise in avoiding pregnancy if they were likely to have an "Rh baby"? A generation ago, much publicity was given to the problem of "Rh babies." This concern resulted from the discovery that a mother with Rh-negative blood who has previously had an Rh-positive baby—one with a different blood factor than she herself possessed—might build up antibodies in her system which would endanger future children. This condition should never be a matter of concern for mothers having their first child, but only those with Rh-negative blood who have given birth to an Rh-positive child. This is only a small percentage of the population, since four out of five women have Rh-positive blood and therefore cannot have an "Rh baby," nor can wives with Rh-negative blood whose husbands also have Rh-negative blood.

But in cases where the wife's blood is Rh-negative and she has already had an Rh-positive baby, a modern obstetrician can handle the case in a routine way so that the future of any new baby will not be endangered. If the wife becomes pregnant, he will examine her blood regularly to make sure that no antibodies are being formed which would affect the child's own blood. Even if there is such an antibody, he can deliver the baby a few weeks earlier than usual, because it is in the last stage of pregnancy that the real danger exists. Moreover, a blood transfusion involving little danger can be given the child immediately after birth, so that the dangerous matter in the blood can be removed.

Similar treatments can be used to lessen the danger to mother or child if the mother has such conditions as diabetes, tuberculosis, heart disease, or high blood pressure. In each case, special treatment will be necessary. For instance, diabetics must follow a careful diet and make special efforts to keep their weight within reasonable limits. A tubercular mother might be given antibiotics which have proved to be highly effective. If a woman with heart disease obtains adequate rest and adheres strictly to rules laid down by a competent doctor, she can also expect to deliver a baby without serious damage. Even extremely high blood pressure can be controlled so that pregnancy will not cause an extreme hazard. In fact, when a woman dies in childbirth today, it is likely that she has either neglected to obtain competent medical care early in her pregnancy and throughout it, or that she neglected to do what her doctor told her.

What can a couple do if a competent doctor warns that the wife is likely to die if she becomes pregnant? Admittedly, this is a heart-rending question. However, it is the one which is asked but rarely, as is proved by the steadily decreasing rate of mothers who die in childbirth.

Nevertheless, there can be no denying that there will be circumstances when, as Pope Pius XII said, "to run the risk of motherhood cannot be demanded" and "where motherhood must be absolutely avoided, and where, on the other hand, the use of sterile period either does not afford a sufficient safeguard or where, for other reasons, it must be discarded." In such a case, His Holiness said, "There is only one thing to do, and that is, to abstain from any complete use of the natural faculty." In other words, the couple must avoid intercourse at any time.

The Pope anticipated criticisms that such a teaching is "inhumane" and beyond the capacity of human beings. His Holiness stated:

"It will be objected that such abstinence is impossible,

that heroism such as this is not feasible. At the present time you can hear and read of this objection everywhere, even from those who, because of their duty and authority, should be of quite a different mind. The following argument is brought forward as proof: No one is obliged to do the impossible and no reasonable legislator is presumed to wish by his law to bind persons to do the impossible. But for married people to abstain for a long time is impossible. Therefore they are not bound to abstain: Divine law cannot mean that.

"In such manner of argument a false conclusion is reached from premises which are only partially true. To be convinced of this, one has simply to reverse the terms of the argument: God does not oblige us to do the impossible. But God obliges married people to abstain if their union cannot be accomplished according to the rules of nature. Therefore, in such cases, abstinence is possible. In confirmation of this argument, we have the doctrine of the Council of Trent which, in the chapter on the necessary and possible observance of the Commandments, referring to a passage in the works of Augustine, teaches: 'God does not command what is impossible, but when He commands, He commands. He warns you to do what you can and to ask His aid for what is beyond your powers, and He gives His help to make that possible for you. . . .'

"To judge men and women of today incapable of continuous heroism is to do them wrong. *In these days, for many reasons—perhaps through dire necessity, or even at times under pressure of injustice—heroism is being practiced to a degree and extent that in times past would have been thought impossible.* Why then, if circumstances

demand it, should this heroism stop at the limits prescribed by passion and the inclinations of nature? It is
obvious that he who does not want to master himself, will
not be able to do so; and he who thinks he can master
himself, relying solely on his own powers and not sincerely and perseveringly seeking divine aid, will be mis-
erably deceived."

8.

The Medical Basis of Fertility Control

LET us suppose that a couple have considered the circumstances of their life and have reached the prudent conclusion that they should not have a child at this time. How, they ask, can they avoid conception with certainty and without using contraceptives?

Since fertility is related to intercourse, the regulation of fertility involves control over the timing and frequency of intercourse. In the monthly cycle of every woman there are only a handful of fertile days. During most of the month it is impossible for her to conceive. By confining intercourse to those sterile days, therefore, the married woman can avoid conception.

This is what we mean by "periodic continence": During the fertile periods of the month the couple abstain. (This practice is popularly called "using the rhythm method." However, this is an inaccurate expression since it is not certain that there is any precise rhythm to ovulation by all women. Furthermore, the term "rhythm" accentuates the biological process rather than the moral virtue being exercised.)

Now let us make one thing clear. The Church, exercising her responsibility as the teacher of men, may declare that periodic continence is morally permissible without at the same time endorsing its use by anyone, certainly without guaranteeing the result intended. For this reason it is erroneous to refer to periodic continence or rhythm as "the Catholic method of birth control." The Church has no method of birth control just as she has no method of fertility. Nature and human choices decide one thing or the other. All that she does, is to point out that, given proper reasons and circumstances, married couples may rightfully use modern knowledge about ovulation to time or space births.

Science and not religion discloses the facts of nature which can help a devoted Christian couple desiring to regulate births. On the basis of present knowledge, however, there are ways for Christians to control the size of their families without putting their marriage and love in jeopardy, and for them to be virtuous at the same time.

The facts to be outlined below are provided for information only. They are not intended to serve as a "how to do it" manual. It cannot be stressed too strongly that a couple seeking to practice periodic continence should consult a qualified doctor who will give them guidance on how to do it effectively. In fact, no one seriously engaged in controlling fertility should consider doing anything without competent counsel. The following information is given to enable you to discuss your problem intelligently with your doctor and to follow his advice.

It is also highly important, we repeat, that you choose

your doctor with great care. For the direction of an informed and interested physician is vital to the success of this kind of family planning, particularly in its early stages. Doctors who know this field of fertility and truly identify with the doctrinal beliefs of their patients have a high incidence of success and merit the affectionate appreciation of countless couples.

However, two kinds of doctors are a menace to troubled people: These are the man who does not know and the man who will not help.

It is amazing but true that many doctors know little about human conception. Whether they are old or young seems to make little difference. We can understand the older man who learned little about ovulation in medical school, but we cannot excuse any doctor not keeping abreast of information vital to the well-being of his patients. This is not merely a matter of book knowledge. A doctor has to learn how ovulation occurs—not just usually, but in this patient or that.

Everyone says that for periodic continence to work, the patient must make the effort. Even more true is this of the doctor. Like specialists of old who fought against insulin for diabetes or penicillin for syphilis because of vested interests in other methods of cure, so today many doctors are addicted to contraception and resist any effort to convince them that determining ovulation can be done effectively and that periodic continence can work for almost all married people.

There are three reasons why you should consult a qualified doctor who is familiar with the latest developments in this field:

1. Many researchers are striving to perfect methods of pinpointing the ovulation period. Your doctor may have, or can get, information which will enable you to practice periodic continence more effectively.

2. Every woman has her own particular pattern. In many cases only an experienced physician is equipped to determine the best method for a particular case.

3. Any couple morally justified in practicing periodic continence should use it in the most efficient way. Especially when there is an urgent need to avoid conception, prudence dictates that the couple get the best possible professional advice they can.

Be sure to select a doctor who is alert to the latest research findings and who also respects Church teachings on this subject. If you live in or near a fairly large city, you probably can find a competent physician by asking at the Catholic hospital for the names of the staff gynecologists or obstetricians. If there is no Catholic hospital in your community, you might obtain the name of a physician qualified in fertility matters from the director of the Family Life Bureau of your diocese. In any event, realize that a doctor who will not accept your moral objections to artificial contraceptives, and pressures you to use them, is not practicing good medicine.

It may well be that, for some time to come, the number of knowledgeable doctors will be too few to handle effectively all the requests being made for counseling in this area. Time, and louder demands by couples in need, will change that. For now some people can be encouraged to turn to another married couple for whom "rhythm" has worked well. Sometimes these experienced lay people surpass doctors in their knowledge of the facts of continent life. Social workers, nurses, educators, midwives, occasionally perfect their knowledge of ovulation for just such situations as this. At all events, seek advice without at the same time relying on hunches, handy rules of thumb, or back-yard gossip.

THE CONCEPTION OF A BABY

The process by which a baby is conceived consists of three separate elements—one in the man's body, one in the woman's body, and a third resulting from the union of both.

For a woman to conceive, she must first of all be of childbearing age and able to produce an ovum or egg, which when fertilized by sperm from the male can be the beginning of a new life.

From about twelve to forty-five years are generally said to be the childbearing years. Each month or so, an ovum is produced in one of the woman's two ovaries. These ovaries are shaped like almonds about an inch and a half long, and are located on each side of the uterus in the pelvic cavity.

The whole area surrounding an egg is just visible to the naked eye as a speck. When an egg leaves the ovary, it passes through an opening in the Graafian follicle in which it developed, and then into a narrow four-inch-long tube (the Fallopian tube) that leads to the uterus. Ovulation occurs when the egg bursts out from the follicle.

So small is an egg that it can be seen only through a powerful microscope. An ordinary soupspoon would hold several million. Yet it contains many of the characteristics

of the mother—the color of her skin, possibly of her hair
and eyes, native talents such as music or art.

While the egg is maturing in the ovary, changes are
taking place in the uterus to accommodate it if it should
become fertilized. The uterus is normally about the size
of a pear and is in about the center of the pelvis. On its
sides are muscles through which many blood vessels run.
After menstruation is completed in each monthly cycle,
the uterus begins to develop a thick, soft lining of blood
vessels which will serve as the home of the fetus if conception occurs.

The egg can be fertilized only by sperm from the male.
These sperm develop in the testicles, two oval-shaped organs which hang below the penis. They are stored in an
organ called the *vas deferens* and at the time of intercourse they pass through the penis and into the vagina.

Doctors estimate that 200 to 500 million sperm are
ejaculated at coitus. A single sperm is about one five-hun-
dredths of an inch long, and cannot be seen by the un-
aided eye. Why should so many million sperm be provided if only one can perform the act of fertilization? One
explanation that has been offered is that sperm, absorbed
in the vagina, contribute to a woman's general well-being.

The distance from the vagina to the Fallopian tubes
is about five inches. Yet it is believed that as many as
several hundred sperm may reach the tube, which is
about the thickness of a hair. Inside the tube, there may
be additional inches to travel, depending upon how far
the egg has traveled from the ovary.

Some medical men believe that fertilization often has
occurred within half an hour of intercourse. This means
that the tiny sperm has moved from the top of the vagina

where it has been deposited, through the uterus, and some distance inside the tube, in less than thirty minutes.

If the sperm make this journey when there is no egg in a Fallopian tube, conception obviously cannot occur. As a general rule, sperm loses its power to fertilize an ovum within seventy-two hours, according to the most conservative authorities. (The consensus of medical opinion puts a forty-eight-hour limitation on the fertilizing power of sperm.) The egg of the woman also has a fertile span of no more than twenty-four hours after leaving the ovary. If it does not encounter a sperm within that time, conception will not occur.

If the egg is not fertilized, it disintegrates. Therefore conception is not possible until the next ovulation. Although some doctors, in trying to explain an unexpected pregnancy, have offered the guess that two ovulations are possible within one menstrual cycle, most modern authorities say that there is no evidence of this, and that for ordinary purposes it is safe to assume that conception will not occur after the egg has disintegrated and that menstruation will follow twelve to sixteen days later.

Thus the period after ovulation is the safest time in the entire cycle. All students of the question stress this fact. Most so-called "failures" seem to result from an unrecognized delay in ovulation. But once the passage of ovulation has been recognized, the woman enters the "safest" time of the month.

A different story begins to unfold if one sperm reaches the egg, burrows through its hard shell covering, and penetrates the core. By God's marvelous plan of reproduction, once the egg is fertilized, no other sperm can enter it.

At that split-second when the sperm penetrates the

ovum and the contribution of the husband and wife are united into a single being, life begins. Although invisible to the eye, it already has within itself much of the story of the infant's life. It tells his sex, because one type of sperm will produce a girl and another a boy. At the moment of fusion, the infant's skin color is determined, the type of his blood, the shape of his nose and jaw, many other physical features as well as his native intelligence and talents such as artistic, literary, or musical ability.

That tiny cell, smaller than a drop of water, is nevertheless a precious being in the sight of Almighty God, one with as much right to life as the father or mother whose union in the act of love produced it.

Inasmuch as qualified doctors believe that the egg loses its vitality within twenty-four hours unless fertilized by the sperm, and that the sperm is fertile no longer than seventy-two hours, actually a woman can be made pregnant only within a four-day period during her monthly cycle, three days before the moment of ovulation and one day after it. If intercourse occurs more than three days before ovulation, the sperm will die before the egg is discharged from the ovary. If intercourse occurs more than twenty-four hours after the egg has been discharged, it, too, will have lost its ability to be fertilized before any sperm reaches the Fallopian tube.

The fertile period may well be shorter than four days. At present it is not possible to determine exactly when these four days are. Further research unquestionably will pinpoint this matter more closely. As mentioned above, this is why it is important to be in constant touch with your doctor, who can be expected to know the latest discoveries. Until science can speak with greater accuracy, however, it would be wise to be cautious and, if anything, to consider the fertile period as being longer than this, rather than shorter.

It is obvious that the successful use of periodic continence depends upon the wife's ability to know when these four days are, which depends upon her knowing when she will ovulate or has ovulated. For then she will know when she is likely to conceive a child and when she is unlikely to do so.

METHODS FOR DETERMINING POTENTIALLY FERTILE DAYS

The search for an accurate way to determine when the fertile period occurs has been carried out in earnest only in relatively recent times. But that there are both fertile and safe times in woman's monthly cycle has been suspected since Biblical days. For example, the ancient Hebrews were deeply concerned with the perpetuation of the race and with following the injunction, "Increase and multiply," which God gave to Adam and Eve. (Genesis, 1:28.) We read in the Book of Leviticus that Jewish women should abstain from intercourse for about twelve days after menstruation. When intercourse was renewed, therefore, it was under conditions when conception would be most likely.

.Until comparatively recent times, it was widely held that the least likely time of conception was during the midpoint of the cycle. Not until the late 1920s was this theory effectively disputed. At that time, two men working independently published reports on investigations which had clearly established that the true safe period was in fact the very time which had generally been supposed to be the fertile period.

The Calendar Method. The verified findings that ovulation time is roughly midway in the menstrual cycle led to the development of what has become known as "the calendar method" of fertility control.

This method is applied as follows: (1.) The wife keeps records of her periods for at least six months and possibly a year, carefully noting how much time elapses each month between the first day of one menstruation and the first day of the next. For example, a woman whose bleeding starts on the first of January and experiences another menstruation on the thirty-first day of January, had a thirty-day cycle that month. (The first day of new bleeding is counted in the new cycle.)

Most women have a fairly regular cycle—one which is regular with them, at least. The woman in our case would after a year likely discern a fairly consistent pattern. For instance, she may find successive cycles of 28, 31, 29, 28, 28, 32, 30, 28, 31, 28, 29, 32. Obviously, the twenty-eight-to-thirty-two-day range constitutes her normal cycle.

The question might be asked legitimately: What about the sexual life of the couple while the woman is collecting this data? The answer depends on the urgency of the situation. Here is something man and wife must work out for themselves, perhaps with some guidance from the family physician. Greater or lesser degrees of abstinence will be necessary.

This suggests the advisability of women, even during the engagement period and certainly during the early years of marriage, making and recording those observations that will be helpful to them later, when circumstances might indicate that family limitation is in order. This knowledge may never be used but it is handy knowledge nonetheless.

(2.) Her next step is to determine the fertile and sterile days in every *future* month. She can do this by making an ordinary monthly calendar.

Let us see what this might look like.

MAY

M 1	M 2	M 3	M 4	M 5	S 6	S 7
S 8	S 9	F 10	F 11	F 12	F 13	F 14
F 15	F 16	F 17	F 18	F 19	F 20	F 21
S 22	S 23	S 24	S 25	S 26	S 27	S 28
M 29	M 30	M 31				

JUNE

		M 1	M 2	3	4

(*IMPORTANT: This is only a sample calendar. No reader must assume that her cycles will follow this pattern.*)

A—Notice first the "M" which stands for menstruation. Using the same case we mentioned above, you see that this woman began this month's menstruation on May 1. How long she menstruates is of little significance because these menstrual days are also sterile (marked "S"). You also notice that she had marked "M" toward the end of the month, because—knowing from her previous record that her cycles run from twenty-eight to thirty-two days —she presumes her next period is likely to begin on May 29, 30, 31, June 1, or 2.

B—Now look at the days she has marked "F." These are her potentially fertile days. How did she determine that these are likely days for her to conceive? To determine this is not so difficult as some people think.

First, every woman should know that ovulation will occur twelve to sixteen days before the onset of the next menstruation. So she counts back sixteen days from Day 29 (the expected beginning of her next cycle). This would be May 13 in the above example. She knows for sure that the four days, May 13, 14, 15, and 16, are likely days for her to ovulate and so marks them "F."

But she knows that her husband's sperm, deposited in advance, holds its fertilizing power up to *three days,* so she marks off May 10, 11, and 12 also as "F" days.

Realizing that her own egg can survive for ONE DAY, she also marks as "F" May 17, since intercourse on May 17 could bring about the fusion of sperm with the ovum that was released the day before.

Now, since her cycles sometimes go to thirty-two days, she has *four more days* to call fertile, since this may be one of her longer months, and so she calls May 18, 19, 20, and 21 also "F" days.

Look again at the above chart and see how simply the potentially fertile days can be identified: Count back *nineteen days* from the beginning of the shortest cycle and you reach the first "F" day. Three successive days are marked "F" to allow for waiting sperm. The next four days for possible ovulation, one day to cover the life-span

of the egg, and as many other days as you get by sub-
tracting the shortest from the longest cycle. In the above
example only four days were added because twenty-eight
from thirty-two days leave four.

All other days are marked "S" or Sterile because conception is not likely to occur. Therefore, those who want
a baby should concentrate intercourse on days marked
"F," while those wishing to avoid conception must restrict
their love-making to days marked "S."

The value of the "calendar method" is that it is fairly
easy for almost everyone to use. Once a wife knows her
own basic menstrual pattern, she can compute her fertile
and sterile periods quickly. Only simple records need be
kept.

This method has enabled most couples to avoid conception for as long as they considered necessary. Many
physicians recommend it when the wife has fairly regular
cycles and the couple would not suffer extreme hardship
if a child were conceived.

However, this system can merely indicate the likely
date of ovulation—it cannot predict it with certainty.
While past records can give an idea of what is likely in
the future, variations may often throw the prediction off.
If a woman has a severe cold, her period may be several
days longer than previous ones of which she has kept
records. Her cycle may be shorter due to pleasant excitement.

One woman had regular cycles of twenty-nine to thirty-
one days over a period of fourteen months. Then both her
parents were killed in an automobile accident. Apparently the shock affected her menstrual pattern; she became pregnant because she had intercourse on a day

which previous calculations indicated was "safe." However, even in such a case, experienced couples make allowances for these interferences.

This method has been used effectively in many parts of the Western world. Its cautious use, however, makes abstention necessary during a large part of the cycle. Young couples who could easily abstain for four or five days may find it more difficult to do so for nine or ten days or longer.

For the more effective use of periodic continence, other methods of calculating the period of fertility may be required. Four techniques, which may enable husbands and wives to cut down on the period of abstinence, have been developed. These are:

"Obvious Ovulation" Method. This can be used only by relatively few women. Some are able to tell exactly when they ovulate, because around midmonth they experience cramps somewhat similar to those which occur when menstruation begins. Some women feel a twinge of pain in the lower abdomen on one side or the other when ovulation occurs. Others note a bloody discharge. (This is not to be confused with menstruation, as it often is.)

The exact causes for these symptoms are not fully understood, but they are mostly due to the indirect effects of hormonal changes. The fact that they occur has been confirmed by numerous researchers. Sometimes a woman experiences these conditions without thinking about them in connection with ovulation. Some were aware of occasional twinges of pain, staining, etc., but never ascertained if there was a pattern to these experiences. When they began to keep records of these symptoms in connection with their menstrual periods, they sometimes discovered that their pains were appearing with regularity fourteen days or so before each menstrual period began. In addition, they often experienced a mucus discharge, cramps, diarrhea, headaches, abdominal pressure, or psychological depression.

A woman who manifests such symptoms has a reliable method of ascertaining when she ovulates, and thus when her fertile period nears its end. If she abstains from intercourse up to three days after experiencing the abdominal pains or noting the show of blood, she is unlikely to conceive at that time. However, by itself, this method is not accurate enough, for it does not tell her when she is going to ovulate. As we have seen, intercourse within seventy-two hours of ovulation may result in conception, since the male sperm may live up to seventy-two hours. Therefore, she will have to use other methods of determining in advance when she will ovulate. In any event, if a woman regularly has symptoms which indicate ovulation, she can cut down the margin of safety which she would otherwise be expected to allow in the half of her cycle before menstruation.

Tes-Tape Method. In recent years, much publicity has been given to the test-tape method of determining ovulation. Since this technique is new, much research remains to be done. The basis of future confidence in test tape rests on the following discoveries: At the fertile time, increased amounts of glucose are secreted into the vagina. Scientists, in attempting to devise a signal of ovulation have used a piece of specially prepared paper—called Tes-Tape—to detect this glucose. Inserted into the vagina by means of a plastic Testor, this paper turns light blue a few days before ovulation and becomes dark blue with ovulation, showing no coloration at all when ovulation is completely passed.

When a woman thinks that her fertile period is impending, she uses this special applicator to insert the test paper. For new patients, this might begin with the end of her menstruation until ovulation has occurred. If, after remaining in the vagina for ten minutes or longer, the test paper is colorless, it is an indication that ovulation will not occur for several days and that intercourse now is unlikely to result in conception. If the paper shows a light blue color, there is some sign that ovulation is about to take place. If it turns a darkish blue, then, according to its inventors, ovulation is occurring or has just occurred and the most likely time for conception is at hand.

Much research remains to be done before the Fertility Testor becomes an adequate tool for ovulation-determination. Sometimes the paper loses its sensitivity. Sometimes it may not be inserted in the right place. And sometimes the dark-blue color may not be a sign of ovulation at all. After all, the color change is due to the presence of glucose. And glucose may be produced in the human body by factors other than ovulation. Even after the paper shows no color, there is still uncertainty as to whether or not ovulation has really passed.

One can only suggest that each woman try this method for herself. For some women it works. When it works, it is a helpful instrument because it shows not only when ovulation is over but, even more importantly, when it is about to occur. Such a development is an advance in knowledge, when it really works.

Body-Temperature Method. This method in many ways is one of the most reliable moral techniques thus far invented for the purposes of periodic continence. It relies on the fact that there is a rise of the hormone progesterone in the body after the egg is discharged from the ovary. With the increase in the progesterone level, the body temperature (granting individual variations) usually rises one full degree Fahrenheit.

Let us see how this works out in practice. The chart on the following two pages of one woman's temperature for the month tells an interesting story.

Note that just prior to menstruation, the woman's temperature is at a high level, usually as much as 98.5°: By the end of menstruation the temperature has fallen to a low level, perhaps below 97.5°. As the cycle progresses, there may be a further decline, although this does not always happen. In any event, notice how following ovulation there is an observable increase in temperature, as much as one degree, to more than 98.0°, a level which is maintained until the next menstruation.

A woman seeking to use this knowledge for purposes of family limitation should take the following steps:

1. She should get the right thermometer. While any thermometer will do, there is a particularly accurate one called *Ovulindex,* purchasable in any drugstore, graded from 96.0° to 100.0° and showing changes of one-tenth of a degree.

2. Each morning, upon awakening and *before* commencing any daily activity (this is very important), she takes her daily temperature. Placing the thermometer under her tongue for five minutes while she reclines in bed is sufficient.

3. After observing her morning temperature *accurately,* she records it immediately and *accurately.* Charts dis-

Ovulindex temperature chart

for use with the Ovulindex thermometer in determining the time and occurrence of ovulation

To obtain an Ovulindex thermometer, show this chart to your regular prescription druggist. He will have it in stock or will quickly get it for you from his wholesaler. Look for the name Ovulindex on the white kit-box and the enclosed 16-page handbook. Every Ovulindex is certified to register *within* 0.1° at *three* test points, 97°, 98°, and 99°. Substitutes do not have this accuracy.

SPECIAL INSTRUCTIONS:

_____

_____ M.D.

The Ovulindex thermometer

Readings and Notes   1960

HOW TO USE THIS CHART: Fill in the dates in advance. As illustrated above, each day make a *little* circle around the number corresponding to your temperature and make notes of signs. Your doctor will interpret your chart for you. To save his time, carefully read the handbook with the Ovulindex; it gives all the little details which will help you to use it successfully and answers common

describes the signs of the fertile time, and illustrates and explains three typical temperature records. Fertility becomes more and more likely each day following the menses until the day when ovulation occurs. Fertility becomes less and less likely each day after ovulation. To increase or reduce the chance of conception, intercourse is timed accordingly.

Physicians may request copies of this chart without charge from:

Linacre Laboratories, Box 1938, New York 17, N. Y.

Copyright 1961, Linacre Laboratories

Ovulindex, Reg. U.S. Pat. Office

Date	Readings and Notes

tributed with the Ovulindex enable her to do this easily.

4. Upon such charts (as the month progresses) she also puts down her menstrual record, carefully noting when menstruation begins. She is expected to note significant changes in her physical condition—for example, if she has had a cold, a fever, or other illness which might affect her temperature.

In the beginning it might not be wise for her to interpret this chart without help. Her family physician might well give her instruction prior to the use of Ovulindex and, then, when she has kept careful records for at least three months, he can analyze these records for her, acquaint himself with her pattern and show her how to read her own chart so that she herself can determine when ovulation has occurred.

The important things to look for are the low level and the high level. The low level tells when ovulation has not yet occurred. Later in the month, persistence of the temperature for THREE DAYS at the high level (for instance, beyond 98.0°) indicates that the fertile time has passed.

The value of the body-temperature method is that it gives more precise information about ovulation. It will usually show when ovulation is delayed. It cuts down on the period of abstinence.

Use of this technique requires some intelligence and care. Some people get easily confused because they are always looking for some sharp rise in temperature, which does not always happen. The only important thing to look for is the beginning of the high phase. While temperature does not predict when ovulation will occur, with skill most women can determine when ovulation is over. Used in conjunction with the calendar method, it can prove very helpful.

Cervix Examination Method. It has been established that definite changes take place in the cervix during the menstrual cycle. By watching these changes, it is possible to determine when ovulation is about to occur or has occurred. A woman can be shown by a doctor how to make this examination and how to interpret what she sees.

In this connection, Dr. Edward F. Keefe, assistant attending obstetrician and gynecologist of St. Vincent's Hospital, New York, states four things:

(1) That at the beginning of the menstrual cycle, the texture of the cervix itself is firm. It becomes progressively softer as ovulation approaches and is "spongy and "rubbery" at the time of ovulation. It becomes increasingly firmer after ovulation and remains that way until menstruation.

(2) The mouth of the cervix is barely open after menstruation. As ovulation approaches, the cervix opens wide so that at the time of ovulation, penetration becomes easy. After ovulation, it begins to close again.

(3) Cervical mucus also undergoes noticeable changes throughout the cycle. Just after menstruation, the amount to be found is scanty and it is thick, sticky, and dark. As ovulation approaches, the amount of mucus increases. Now it becomes jellylike and ropy in texture. During ovulation, it is voluminous. The texture is watery and has a clear egg-white color. (By way of parenthesis, these data manifest the wonder of God's design. All these signs show how during ovulation the woman's body offers the least resistance to penetration and conception.)

(4) Soon after ovulation, the amount of mucus begins to decrease, its texture becomes gummy again, and it takes on a cloudy, uniform appearance. By the time menstruation is about to begin, the quantity is scanty and the mucus assumes an opaque, yellow appearance.

In a report published by the *Bulletin of the Sloane Hospital for Women*, Dr. Keefe states that "this method, while not ideal, is an advance. It could become common knowledge that if a woman finds her cervix flaccid, gaping and streaming with mucus, there is a chance of conception and in the absence of these signs, there is less or no chance."

Probably every woman finds one or more of these methods difficult or unsatisfactory. However, if she maintains a calendar record of her menstrual history and familiarizes herself with the other techniques, she probably can piece together enough information to become highly proficient in working out a suitable pattern of childbearing.

SPECIAL FACTORS WHICH MAY AFFECT FERTILITY

The age of the woman, her emotional responses and living habits, whether she has recently given birth, and other factors may affect the regularity of her cycle.

Girls generally have irregular patterns for several years after they begin menstruating until they reach about age twenty. Then they usually "settle down" and experience some kind of regularity. As they approach menopause, their cycles become irregular.

For several months after birth or miscarriage, a woman

should not be surprised if her periods are longer or shorter than those to which she has been accustomed. It may be several months after giving birth before a woman menstruates. If she breast-feeds her infant, she may have several fifty- or sixty-day cycles. After she discontinues breast-feeding, she may have a few highly irregular periods before resuming a consistent cycle.

Factors suspected of making a particular cycle longer than usual include an illness with a high fever, a heavy or prolonged cold, unusual physical exertion (of the type required in moving from one house to another, for example), and serious emotional disturbances, such as that which might be caused by the death of a loved one or by excessive worry. A woman taking medicines (especially hormone preparations) also may be susceptible to irregularities.

Drastic changes in living habits, such as moving from a very cold climate to a warm one or undertaking a drastic dieting program, likewise are thought to affect the length of the cycles of some women. Changes in sexual habits also are suspect. For instance, striking irregularities have been reported immediately after marriage, or upon a husband's return after a long absence. In some cases, a woman's sexual excitement may cause a secretion of hormones which results in an earlier-than-usual ovulation.

In addition, a small number of women may be much more fertile than others, and for them ordinary guides may not apply. It is thought possible, for example, that their body conditions may be such that sperm retain the ability to fertilize much longer than usual.

The wife who would use periodic continence effectively must study herself to understand how such conditions affect her. In the final analysis, she must decide for herself when she may be fertile. A doctor may show her how to make various tests which indicate whether she may be fertile or sterile, but she must make final decisions in the light of her own knowledge of herself.

HOW RELIABLE IS PERIODIC CONTINENCE?

It is obvious that some risk of pregnancy, however slight, is involved whenever a couple engage in normal intercourse. There is no *absolutely certain* way of avoiding conception when there is coitus. Even proponents of contraceptives admit this about every artificial method. When we speak of "reliability," therefore, we speak in a relative way.

Since pregnancy results from intercourse and abstaining from intercourse is the main feature of the "rhythm method," it follows that a husband and wife who abstain will not have children. As a practical matter, of course, a husband and wife will engage in sexual relations but as a general principle we can say that the more cautious they are in having relations at a time when the wife may be fertile, the more effective will they be in limiting their family size.

Many doctors—non-Catholic as well as Catholic—have reported that periodic continence, when practiced as directed, has good reliability. For instance, two researchers on the National Committee of Maternal Health, Inc.— Christopher Tietze, M.D. and Robert G. Potter, Jr., Ph.D.— have reported in the *American Journal of Obstetrics and Gynecology* that the theoretic effectiveness of periodic continence based only on the calendar method as described above, "is roughly comparable to that of the diaphragm or condom." When this method is followed consistently, after the woman's cycles have been recorded for a year, they stated, there is a "90 per cent chance of avoiding pregnancy for five to ten years." A couple who deviate from this method by "taking a chance" and shortening the period of abstinence will naturally assume a greater risk of pregnancy. Those who lengthen the period of abstinence will be even safer.

Dr. J. G. H. Holt, a Dutch physician, who says that he has observed the practice of periodic continence by thousands of women, states that use of the temperature method provides "an unequaled guarantee of safety." Dr. I. E. Georg of Vienna states that "generally excellent results" can be achieved by this method when it is followed as suggested. Dr. Alan F. Guttmacher, a medical spokesman for the Planned Parenthood Federation of America, places the "rhythm method" about midway in effectiveness among methods of family limitations. He regards it as less effective than oral pills, cervical caps, diaphragms, condoms, and jellies or creams, but more effective than suppositories, vaginal foam tablets, and vaginal douches.

It stands to reason that the more information a husband and wife have about the ways to determine the fertile days, the greater understanding they have of the wife's particular reponse patterns, and the stronger motivation and discipline they have to abstain when necessary, the more likely that they will achieve the results intended.

The important point which should never be overlooked is that the effectiveness of periodic continence depends to the greatest extent upon *the understanding by the wife and husband of the circumstances that govern their individual case.* It is of no value to know that 85 per cent of wives are sufficiently regular to use the "Calendar Method" successfully if this particular wife is the one woman in ten who has a pattern of such inconsistency that the only guidance this method can recommend is total abstinence. However, if such a wife were to study her cycle carefully and watch for the typical signs of ovulation, making use of the simple cervix examination for clues as to the onset of ovulation and the temperature charts which indicate when ovulation has passed, she probably can come to a reasonably workable understanding of when her fertile and sterile periods begin and end. Only by spending the time required to study her own particular circumstances can she understand how to make periodic continence work effectively for her.

Not long ago, a young woman appeared at the office of a prominent Catholic obstetrician. Her first words were: "Doctor, I think I'm going to have a rhythm baby."

The physician determined that she was pregnant. At the conclusion, he said: "The signs indicate indeed that you will become a mother. But what is this about rhythm?"

The patient explained that she and her husband had been practicing periodic continence for a year and a half. She insisted that they had faithfully "followed the rules," as she termed it, to avoid conception.

The doctor asked if she had maintained records which would enable her to determine when her sterile period would be. She replied airily: "I used to put things down on paper, but after a while I decided it wasn't necessary. We just figured out when ovulation would take place, and abstained for two days before and two days afterwards."

Because of his interest in the effectiveness of periodic continence and the reason why it sometimes fails to achieve the intended results, the doctor asked his patient to recall the date of her last few menstrual periods and the time she had decided her fertile period to be. In examining these records, he was able to show her that she had made a mistake of two days in her calculations and that she and her husband had had marital relations on the day conception was most likely to occur.

Some couples who think they are correctly practicing periodic continence are doing nothing of the sort. It is not unusual for a wife to reason something like this:

"My regular monthly period has been twenty-eight days regularly. Occasionally I have gone to thirty days, and sometimes twenty-six, but lately it has been around twenty-eight. Now I read some time ago that a woman with a twenty-eight-day cycle would be fertile from the thirteenth to the fifteenth day. We'll just abstain on those days, and we'll be safe."

The wife who reasons this way is not making use of the scientific information available to her. She is doing something which no one has ever recommended. Through ignorance or an unwillingness to learn how to use the facts of nature to fit her particular circumstances, she is doing little more than taking a chance that intercourse will not result in conception. However, if she becomes pregnant, she might say that "the method doesn't work."

We have every reason to share the hope expressed by Pope Pius XII that an even more secure method of using periodic continence may soon be developed for those very irregular or emotional women who do not now find present techniques sufficiently accurate. It is worth noting that advocates of contraception have long put forward as their ideal, a method that would be at once reasonably trustworthy, easy for anyone to use after a few simple instructions, harmless, and inexpensive enough so that couples in economic need could use it. There is every likelihood that scientific research will enable the practice of periodic continence to meet all these requirements.

GOOD COMMUNICATIONS NEEDED

The following points are important for a husband and wife to bear in mind in order to practice periodic continence successfully:

They should have good communication between themselves. They should be able to talk to each other with complete freedom and frankness, so that they can agree upon objectives and techniques and understand what particular physical and emotional difficulties they may encounter.

If a couple candidly discuss their problems, each will understand the other's reasons for having or not having another child. Sometimes a couple practice periodic continence without this clear understanding. A wife may believe it is not prudent to become pregnant because she fears her husband will be unable to support the new life. On the other hand, the husband may believe that his income will be substantially higher when the baby arrives. He may think that his wife really wishes to defer pregnancy because she fears her health will not be good enough to bear, and care for, a child. If husband and wife keep things to themselves and do not reveal their thoughts to the other, they often may find themselves working at cross-purposes.

When a husband and wife understand why they are doing something, they develop a common strength to help them achieve their objective. This is especially true if their motivation is worthy and idealistic—in this case, if they practice periodic continence not to satisfy selfish instincts but rather to make any necessary sacrifices for the well-being of the other. For instance, a husband sincerely interested in his wife's physical well-being who knows she should not become pregnant will be more inclined to exercise self-control than would a man who thinks his own desires should be satisfied regardless of the cost to his wife.

In addition to understanding clearly their own motivation, husband and wife should discuss practical difficulties that may arise as the days of abstinence approach.

Some couples may find it difficult to discuss such matters frankly. This condition is a holdover from the days when sex was generally considered to be "dirty," and when it was thought shameful even for married persons to talk about sexual relations to each other. Fortunately, this puritanism is uncommon among young couples today. In fact, some moderns tend to go to the other extreme, in which sex is discussed openly, not only with one's partner but with any friend, acquaintance, or stranger who cares to listen. Ideally, sex should be treated publicly with the restraint that its holy nature demands, but also with candor by husband and wife together.

The reader who is inclined to regard discussion of physical relationships as being out-of-bounds, may be benefited by doing some careful, unemotional thinking about this matter. Obviously sex is not "dirty." How can it be, when it was created by Almighty God Himself as the only way in which the propagation of the human race can be accomplished? It is well to remember that the marital act has been the way by which every human being from the dawn of history—including the Blessed Virgin, the Apostles and the saints—has been conceived. Moreover, it was God Himself Who associated pleasure with married love, Who created sexual organs and the responses that naturally follow stimulation. Therefore, using what God has created is good, and discussing it is good where the end result is growth in married love, responsible conduct, and virtuous living.

Because it is so important for them to be able to communicate about their private relationships, Catholics intending to marry are urged to attend Pre-Cana conferences held in their diocese. At these conferences, generally conducted by a priest, a doctor, and lay panel, the couple may learn to rid themselves of false ideas passed on to them by parents or environment, and they will be encouraged to discuss their needs, aspirations, and experiences with each other. Indeed, it has been found that the ability to discuss frankly all areas of mutual interest in marriage insures that the husband and wife will grow closer together with the years.

If the Pre-Cana experience was not possible for a husband and wife, we recommend Cana conferences which are now held especially for married men and women in an increasing number of dioceses. It might also be wise to discuss the difficulties with an understanding priest, a competent Catholic psychologist, or other marriage counselor. Such an authority may be able to assure a scrupulous husband or wife that it is often less in harmony with Our Lord's teachings to maintain reticence than to speak with the aim of improving marital relations and the marriage itself.

Particularly in the early stages, a wife must keep careful records indicating when her fertile period can be expected. Since the success of this method requires accurate knowledge of when the fertile days occur, it is necessary to spend time to take temperature readings or whatever other steps are required.

This point should be obvious. Nevertheless, it is frequently overlooked. As a result, the results achieved by couples who have practiced periodic continence are not as good as they could be. In fact, it will often be found that when this method "fails," it does so not because of any defect in the method itself, but rather because of errors of omission or commission which couples have made in applying it.

Husband and wife must learn to recognize and avoid circumstances which are likely to heighten their desire for intercourse. For example, some persons react to an alcoholic drink or two with an increased sense of affection. After an evening with a few cocktails or highballs, a couple may feel disposed towards love-making. Men and women who are shy and modest by nature often discover that a few drinks release their inhibitions. It is well known that alcohol increases the desire for intercourse.

If a husband or wife finds that alcohol stimulates sexual desires so much that they are difficult to control at certain times, they may have to abstain from drinking as well when they must abstain from sex. This might

mean arranging their social life with the need for abstinence in mind, which for the average couple is not as
difficult as it might seem. If a wife is planning a party or
a night out with her husband which might involve drinking, she might find it just as convenient to set the date
for a few days before the expected fertile period, or a
few days after it, instead of at the very time when she
would be fertile.

Advocates of artificial methods of contraception often
make much of the fact that couples trying to practice
periodic abstinence may find that their intentions have
weakened after they have had a few drinks. While this
is true, it is also true that every artificial method also
requires some form of self-discipline. It is just as easy for
a person to fail to use an artificial device properly when
under the influence of drink.

The couple practicing periodic continence must also
recognize which acts of affection are harmless, in that
they do not create a strong desire for intercourse, and
which actions can easily lead to urges which are as difficult to check.

The kiss which husband and wife exchange as he
leaves for work or returns at night, the holding of hands,
the good-night kiss—these are not overlaid with sexual
connotations. On the other hand, prolonged kissing, fon-
dling, and other acts of familiarity tend to create desire
and—unless kept under strict control—may soon grow out
of bounds. Insofar as morality is concerned, a couple may
engage in any affectionate acts which either lead to intercourse or can be discontinued without leading either or
both partners to solitary impurity. In other words, acts of
affection by the married, terminated short of intercourse,

are perfectly permissible and indeed are recommended, since there can never be any solid reason for a married couple living like "brother and sister." But they must know themselves and each other and the limitations imposed on their love-making on certain occasions by their deliberate decision not to have a child at this time.

Ways of showing affection which to one couple may be entirely bereft of sexual meaning may be highly charged for another. For instance, some persons can engage in a great amount of kissing without creating strong desires. In others, a gentle contact between the lips, the whiff of perfume, or the accidental brush of bodies may cause powerful stirrings. Therefore a third person cannot say that this or that action should be avoided. But a general principle can be laid down: The couple should study themselves and learn to recognize the circumstances which will make it difficult for them to practice abstinence. To the best of their ability, they should then avoid such circumstances.

While refraining from too-passionate activities which might create desires which cannot be satisfied, the periodically continent couple should also avoid the extreme of limiting their demonstrations only to times when the wife is sterile.

The danger that expressions of love might be turned on and off like a faucet has led to charges that the couples who periodically abstain tend to "make love by the c̣ endar." This need not be so because, as we have the act of sex is but one of many ways in whic' and wife may indicate their love. Simple act᷉ in the home, gentle words of appreciatiᷛ and caresses—these should not be neᷰ᷈ least of all when it is not feasible to manifest love in the sexual way.

It should not be overlooked that if a couple suppress their normal instincts for affection during some part of the month, their ability to express themselves in a loving way may be impaired permanently. Recently a wife told a marriage counselor this story:

"When Tom and I were first married, he was filled with affection for me and showed it to such an extent that I was sometimes embarrassed by it. He had a powerful sexual drive, and his affectionate acts often were a preliminary to intercourse.

"We had three children, and then Tom lost his job. For a year, we were on relief. Naturally we felt that we could not bring another child into the world, and we began to abstain on days when I might be fertile.

"For many months after things began to go poorly for us, Tom remained his old affectionate self. But then, I noticed that he was becoming noticeably cooler to me on days when intercourse might lead to pregnancy. He was obviously afraid to show affection for fear that his desires might get out-of-hand.

"But unfortunately aloofness became a habit with him. And when we had intercourse, it was not like before. Now it was almost entirely a physical process—something that seemed to lack emotional content. For us, the need to 'make love tonight' took the emotional satisfaction out of intercourse."

This woman's experience can be avoided if a couple recognize these dangers, and develop nonsexual ways of expressing their love for each other in order to retain the emotional spontaneity of the act when they do perform it.

Husbands and wives should thoroughly understand the factors which generally create a desire for intercourse in the opposite sex. In his chapter, "A Catholic Doctor Looks at Marriage," in the *Catholic Marriage Manual,* Dr. Bernard J. Pisani outlines the differences in this way:

"The man is more easily aroused. He requires little direct stimulation to create an interest in the sex union. In fact, he may feel desire as the result of the very sight of his wife or the smell of her perfume, or a toss of her head or even a glance that is warm and affectionate. His wife responds more slowly, and is affected by a different type of stimulus. Tenderness, gentleness of touch, and consideration by her husband are of paramount importance. Whereas his arousal is most often achieved by physical stimuli, hers is achieved by emotional ones as well.

"A husband generally may be stimulated to desire intercourse at any time of day, week, or month, even at times when he is ill. His wife's desire, on the other hand, tends to be affected by cycles. Her responses depend to some extent upon the balance or interplay of hormones in her system. As these vary at different stages of her menstrual cycle, her desire rises and falls accordingly. Many women have a more powerful sex urge on the day preceding menstruation than at other times; others reach a maximum intensity of desire immediately after menstruation; still others desire marital relations most keenly during their period of ovulation—about midway in the cycle."

In order to practice periodic continence effectively is necessary to recognize these responses as the affect the partner. A wife will avoid actions w knows from experience are likely to arouse b and he will refrain from actions which are her. In some cases, however, an easily aroused person may have to develop greater self-control. A husband who is unusually susceptible to perfume may not be entirely within his rights in asking his wife to refrain from using it entirely during her fertile period. He may have to learn to condition his responses in a different way. In fact many husbands will be required to practice greater self-discipline than they have been accustomed to.

The difficulties involved in periodic continence are very real indeed. But they do not justify the use of artificial methods. It is frequently ignored that the difficulties involved in the use of contraceptives are not small. Contraception suffers all the defects of artificiality. Each particular technique has certain specific defects which tend to make the act of intercourse less natural, less spontaneous, and less safe than it would be otherwise.

For example, the use of the most widely popular contraceptives, the condom, takes much of the spontaneity out of the act. As generally used, it requires an awkward interruption to the act of love-making. Moreover, contraceptionists themselves admit that the barrier created between the man and woman makes it difficult to achieve the sense of union which is the very nature of the act. There is also a very considerable danger that some semen will be accidentally discharged into the vagina.

Other contraceptives, such as the diaphragm and pessary, must be worn by the woman. These, too, create a barrier between the husband and wife unintended by God. Since these pieces of equipment must be inserted with extreme care to prevent semen from traveling into the upper canal, there is always an element of uncertainty in their use—a factor which often creates tension when the couple should be most relaxed.

When a douche is used in an effort to destroy semen in the vagina, the work of contraception must be done by the woman after intercourse is complete. This is certainly no satisfactory end to conjugal love. Some non-Catholic marriage counselors have mentioned the resentment felt by wives who return to the scene of their love-making, wide-awake, while their husbands are sound asleep.

Regardless of what "modern" couples may say, the sexual act is a truly complete union of two in one flesh only when no barrier is placed between the man and woman. All human beings sense this even if they refuse to admit it. The woman who must use some means to reject her husband's seed is aware that the act of love—which should be an act of giving and receiving—has been frustrated.

A few years ago, a young widow who had been born a Protestant entered the Church and married a Catholic. Referring to her sexual experiences, she said: "During my first marriage, before entering the Church, I used contraceptives regularly. They were effective, but I winced every time I used them. I realized that it was an unnatural act, because God made man and woman to give of themselves without holding back. Using contraceptives always made me feel I was not giving of myself freely in love. Only when I remarried in the Church and gave up all contraceptives did I feel that I was a complete woman."

DOES BREAST-FEEDING PREVENT PREGNANCY?

In older days, many people believed that a mother would not become pregnant again as long as she nursed her baby. It is not possible to say, even yet, how much truth there is in this belief. It is a fact, however, that the typical Christian family of the last century—before birth-control devices were used—generally consisted of about six children. In studying the histories of these families, you will find too often to be a mere coincidence that the children are spaced about two years apart. In such families, of course, mothers usually nursed their infants, because "formula feeding" had not been developed on a wide scale.

The tradition that a mother will not conceive during lactation—while she is breast-feeding her infant—goes back to ancient times. Many tribes had taboos against intercourse during this time.

But there is also some evidence that the woman who breast-feeds is least likely to conceive again for a time, depending on the length of the breast-feeding. In fact, pregnancies among nursing mothers are relatively rare in the early months after childbirth. The percentage, however, increases month by month. The best that most obstetricians say for lactation is that, as a means of avoiding conception, individual determinations must be made.

There are no moral objections to the use of breast-feeding even if the intention is to space birth thereby. This is the natural way designed by God for the mother to supply nourishment to her infant. Breast-feeding also has proved psychological value for the baby. Psychiatrists emphasize that an infant has just gone through one of the greatest shocks he will possibly experience—the sudden ejection, from the warm and secure home he has known for nine months, into a strange and difficult world where he will be subjected to hunger, pain, and cold he has never experienced before. But when his mother encloses him in her arms, she helps give him a new sense of security that makes this transition period less shocking.

Insofar as avoiding conception is concerned, the nursing mother does nothing to impede the course of nature, nor does she use any artificial means to prevent the union of semen with her ovum.

A woman who plans to breast-feed her child should advise her doctor of her intentions before the baby is born. While physicians generally approve of the practice, they sometimes advise against it if they think the mother might be unable to supply enough milk of the type the baby needs. A relaxed, easygoing woman generally can provide more milk than one who is nervous and high strung by nature. But much of the opposition to breast-feeding, as an instrument of nutrition or a means of postponing pregnancy, is the result of the modern assembly-line way of bringing children into the world. Doctors, nurses, and sometimes mothers themselves do not want to be bothered. Other woman, however, have found it not only a consoling experience but a good way of baby-spacing.

HELP FOR CHILDLESS COUPLES

Scientific discoveries already made to help fix the exact time of a woman's fertile period are valuable not only to couples who cannot have more children, but also to those who want to conceive but have been unable to do so. It has been estimated that about one couple in ten cannot conceive a child when they engage in marital relations on a "hit or miss" basis. These couples are said to be infertile. Another couple in ten—or 10 per cent of the population—may have one or two children but are unable to conceive more.

There may be many reasons for a couple's inability to conceive. In perhaps three out of every five such cases, the cause lies within the female. She may not be delivering an egg which will survive to be fertilized by the male sperm. She may be deficient in thyroid, so that fertilization does not occur or there is a miscarriage if it does. Her body may lack hormones that the embryo requires to develop properly. Or there may be a blocking of the Fallopian tubes which prevents the egg from traveling through to the uterus where it may be fertilized.

The male is thought to be the cause of sterility in about two cases out of five. His sperm may be defective either in quality or quantity. As we have noted, the average ejaculation includes about 300 million sperm. If an ejaculation contains less than fifty million, many doctors think that the chance of conception is slight. Moreover, if the husband has recently been seriously ill, suffered serious emotional upsets or extreme fatigue, or has flagrantly overindulged in alcohol or tobacco, the sperm's ability to travel to the uterus may be greatly lessened.

Quite possibly, infertility may often lie in the fact that intercourse does not occur when it is most likely to result in conception, or that the pair do not copulate when other conditions are most favorable for pregnancy.

The wife who is unable to conceive would be well-advised to keep all the charts and records recommended earlier in this chapter so that she might determine the day most likely for conception. She and her husband should make it a practice to refrain from intercourse for perhaps a week before this day. They should also try to get a maximum amount of rest and to avoid excesses of alcohol or tobacco. Conditions may then be as favorable as possible.

Although a couple need not seek a doctor's help if they cannot conceive a child in the normal course of events, an appreciation of the vocation of marriage will cause Catholics to obtain competent medical advice. Doctors generally say that a couple may assume that they are infertile if they have vainly tried to conceive a child within eighteen months. Any couple who have gone this period would be wise to consult a fertility expert, because fertility decreases with age, and the longer they wait the less likely success will be.

Using legitimate techniques which modern medicine has developed, many childless couples have been enabled to have one or more children. Their success in achieving parenthood is indeed a cause for joy. For just as family limitation is legitimate when legitimate means are used and legitimate reasons for its practice exists, so too are legitimate efforts to have children.

However, sometimes it happens that in God's Providence parenthood will be denied even to the most worthy people. They try. Doctors help. But nothing seems to work. Here we are dealing with the mystery of life. Here we run into the frequently unanswerable question, "Why?" Facing the agony of sterility, some Christian couples seek children through adoption, others channel their parental energies into the service of the Church, the community, and their own extended family. Basic to all these legitimate ways of fulfilling one's aspirations is the ability of Christians with God's grace to resign themselves to the Cross Christ has asked them to carry for the benefit of their own or someone else's redemption.

Of course, some personalities become bitter when life does not go their way. Not only do they complain, but insist on using illegitimate and immoral ways of getting what they want. Some women, for example, commit adultery. Coming into vogue in our society, on the other hand, is a more devilish form of illegitimate parenthood. I refer to the "test tube baby" which derives from artificial insemination. Failing to assist couples to realize fertility through proper means, many doctors do not hesitate to recommend that a particular wife allow herself to be inseminated artificially, sometimes with the seed of her husband, sometimes with the seed of an anonymous donor!

In other words, male semen is first secured, most frequently by masturbation, deposited into a receptable, and later emptied into the woman's vagina. Such is the wonder of modern science that babies can be conceived this way.

But is this procedure morally right?

Obviously, the commitment of Christian marriage precludes conception that involves a third party. This smacks of adultery. And the very meaning of human marriage itself makes artificial insemination with the husband's seed equally immoral. After all, a husband is not a steed, nor the wife a brood mare, nor the home a stud farm. The marriage act is not merely a transmission belt for seed. The family is not a biological laboratory. Marriage, among humans in general and among Christians in particular, involves the union of persons "in one flesh." It is much more than the union of two seeds. Spouses are ordained to love each other in a personal way. To merge two seeds without the natural act of husband and wife does violence to marriage itself and is an abuse of scientific technique which, whatever its value for animal husbandry, may not be used for human procreation. This is why Pope Pius XII in 1949 said: "Artificial Insemination is something which must not just be regarded with extreme reserve, but must be utterly rejected." And this holds true whether the husband or a stranger is the donor.

Sensitive Christians who give thought to this matter will agree even if their convictions result in continued childlessness and even though less scrupulous counselors laugh at them.

9.

The Providence of God

NO ONE can deny that a couple must be prepared for heroic effort at times if they wish to lead truly Christian lives. Life will not always be soft for the man and woman who choose to have a large family and to educate it in accordance with present standards. The couple who limit the size of their family in a legitimate way by observing periodic continence need backbone. The road for the Christian couple is not and has never been the easiest one to travel—let us not minimize that fact. From the first days in the catacombs, adherence to the teachings of Christ has always cost its believers more sacrifice and hardships than pagans have been willing to pay. When Jesus announced the institution of the Eucharist to his disciples, many turned away, saying: "This is a hard saying, who can listen to it?" (John, 6:61.) The New Testament also tells us that a certain ruler asked Jesus what he must do to gain eternal life. Jesus told him to "sell all that thou hast, and give to the poor, and thou shalt have treasure in heaven; and come follow me." (Luke, 18:18–23.) The man was unable to follow Our Lord's advice and teaching and "was much grieved."

In the early days of the Church, many of the first Christians had to face persecution or death for their beliefs. Yet Christianity could not have survived the Roman terror unless they were willing to live up to all of the difficult teachings of Our Lord. In fact, it was the example of self-sacrifice and love for one another that the Christians showed to the pagans that enabled the Church to grow.

Down through the centuries, Catholics often have had to make great sacrifices for their beliefs. Often they had to face choices even more difficult than those which confront couples in the Western world today. From our own experience, we can recall the sacrifices in time, energy, and material comforts made for us by our own parents.

Actually, one cannot claim to be a true Christian unless one endures the hardships that the genuine belief in the principles of his father involves. It is generally true that a thing is worth what it costs; if it were easy to be a Christian, our religion would have little merit for us. But the practice of Christianity is love in the concrete. The Christian must make a sacrifice in fulfilling Our Lord's instruction to love our neighbor as ourselves. There is a sacrifice in attending Mass on Sunday, in performing the duties of our religion, in remaining honest when the tendency is to get away with what you can, and so on.

When a Christian receives the Sacrament of Confirmation, he becomes a soldier in the Army of Christ. This is not mere rhetoric. It is hard fact.

In the armies of nations, a soldier does not lead an especially difficult life in peacetime. He generally has enough food, warm shelter, many opportunities for recreation and relaxation. One would not say that he proves himself by being a good soldier under such conditions. Rare is the medal given to a soldier for his activities during peace. The true test comes only in battle. It would be a disreputable soldier—one worthy of the scorn of his companions—who deserted to the enemy at the first sign of trouble. A soldier is expected to endure difficulties. He is expected to answer the call to battle.

No less is expected of those who have enrolled themselves in the Army of Christ through Confirmation. In the face of the enemy, the Christian has no choice: He *must* stand up for his principles. When some of Our Lord's disciples deserted Him because they thought His way of life was too hard, Jesus turned to His apostles and asked, "Do you also wish to go away?" Simon Peter gave the answer that every Christian must give: "Lord, to whom shall we go? Thou hast words of eternal life." (John, 6:67–69.)

But difficult as the road may be for the Christian at times, it is never so difficult that he cannot endure it with God's help. Jesus said: "Come to me, all you who labor and are burdened, and I will give you rest. Take my yoke upon you, and learn from me, for I am meek and humble of heart; and you will find rest for your souls. For my yoke is easy, and my burden light." (Matthew, 11:28–30.) Once the Christian knows why he is making his sacrifices, and once he makes them in a desire to conform to the will of God, he discovers that they become easier to bear.

The fact is that Christians are living lives of selfless sacrifice all around us. Such lives of true devotion are being lived by a couple I know with six children in a city apartment. They have willingly foregone many material comforts which their friends enjoy. Nevertheless they are giving their children a greater gift than money can possibly buy—the gift of their constant love and guidance. Such lives are being lived by another couple with two children who are courageously observing prolonged periodic abstinence in order to avoid a future pregnancy which, doctors have told them, might result in the mother's death. Such lives are being lived by a wife and her husband, a naval officer who has been sent to a distant country where wartime conditions prevail. They are practicing the principles of Christian chastity for the several years during which they have been separated. Such lives are also being lived by the sterile wife who is unable to have children for reasons which God alone knows, but who is devoting herself to the service of others by teaching young children in a kindergarten of a parochial school. Inasmuch as lives like these are being lived all about us, nothing could be farther from the truth than that living of Christian principles is "too hard." For all about us we can see heroes and heroines who respond to the call.

In fact, to be Christians, we must be prepared to practice acts of heroism every day of our lives. Our Lord said, "If anyone wishes to come after Me, let him deny himself, and take up his cross, and follow Me." (Matthew, 16: 24.) It is no exaggeration to say that the Christian must decide, each day, whether he is following the way of Our Lord or the way of the crowd.

A man stood at an airline ticket counter, buying a ticket for himself and his son. The ticket clerk pointed out that the son could go half fare if he were under twelve years of age, but the boy was just a few days past his twelfth birthday. Without hesitation, his father told the truth—although a "little lie" could have saved him fifty dollars.

When friends learned what had happened, they told the father that it would have been just as easy to say the boy was eleven. The father replied: "I have spent twelve years trying to teach my son to be a good Christian. What kind of an example would I set if my teachings were not worth more than fifty dollars?"

Christian couples must make similar decisions when facing temptations in their married life. When confronted with questions of their sexual relationships, they must ask whether they are Christians or not. If we believe in God and in the teaching authority of the Church, we have no alternative: We *must* act in accord with Christian principles, regardless of the sacrifice it may entail. But Christians must also believe that God will give us the help to carry successfully any burden which may be placed upon us.

The Christian must believe this because in entering the vocation of marriage, he is doing God's work. The priest on the marriage altar promises that the couple who follow the principles of Our Lord will be given all the graces they need to fulfill their role in life.

A Christian parent must also believe that in doing God's work he can receive all the help necessary to enable him to do a good job. It has been said that the most important attribute you can have as you undertake the responsibilities of married life is faith that God will do His part if you do yours. Read the Gospels carefully and you may be astonished at their large number of references to the all-important virtue of faith. For example, consider these words of Our Lord: "Therefore I say to you, do not be anxious for your life, what you shall eat; nor yet for your body, what you shall put on. Is not the life a greater thing than the food, and the body than the clothing? Look at the birds of the air: they do not sow, or reap, or gather into barns; yet your heavenly Father feeds them. Are not you of much more value than they? But which of you being anxious about it can add to his stature a single cubit?

"And as for clothing, why are you anxious? Consider how the lilies of the field grow; they neither toil nor spin, yet I say to you that not even Solomon in all his glory was arrayed like one of these. But if God so clothes the grass of the field, which flourishes today but tomorrow is thrown into the oven, how much more you, O you of little faith!

"Therefore do not be anxious, saying, 'What shall we eat?' or, 'What shall we drink?' or, 'What are we to put on?' (for after all these things the Gentiles seek); for your Father knows that you need all these things." (Matthew, 6:25-32.)

St. Matthew also tells us that when Our Lord entered Capharnaum, a centurion came to him saying that his servant was grievously ill. Our Lord said that He would cure him. The centurion answered: "Lord, I am not worthy that Thou shouldst come under my roof; but only say the word, and my servant will be healed." Our Lord marveled at his faith, and said to him: "Go thy way; as thou has believed, so be it done to thee." (Matthew, 8: 5-13.)

A woman who had been suffering from hemorrhage for

twelve years came up behind Jesus and touched the tassel of his cloak, saying to herself, "If I touch but His cloak, I shall be saved." But Our Lord saw her, and said, "Take courage, daughter, Thy faith hath saved thee." And the woman was restored to health from that moment. (Matthew, 9:20–22.)

Another time, two blind men followed Jesus and cried out: "Have pity on us, Son of David!" Jesus said to them, "Do you believe that I can do this to you?" They answered Him, "Yes, Lord." Then He touched their eyes, saying, "Let it be done to you according to your faith." And they were healed. (Matthew, 9:27–30.)

Still another time, in speaking with His disciples Our Lord made this flat promise: "Amen I say to you, if you have faith like a mustard seed, you will say to this mountain, 'Remove from here'; and it will remove; and nothing will be impossible to you." (Matthew, 17:19.)

And still another time, Jesus said: "All things whatever you ask for in prayer, believe that you shall receive, and they shall come to you." (Mark, 11:24.)

The Christian with true belief will say, as did St. Paul in his epistle to the Philippians: "I can do all things in Him who strengthens me." (Philippians, 4:13.) And also as St. Paul wrote to the Romans: "If God is for us, who is against us?" (Romans, 8:31.)

Here is ample proof indeed that the Christian must always believe that it is possible to live his married life in full accord with the purposes God had in mind when He instituted the sacrament. As Pope Pius XI said in his encyclical *"Casti Connubii"*:

"There is no possible circumstance in which husband and wife cannot, strengthened by the grace of God, fulfill faithfully their duties and preserve in wedlock their chastity unspotted. This truth of Christian faith is expressed by the teachings of the Council of Trent. 'Let no one be so rash as to assert that which the Fathers of the Council have placed under anathema, namely, that there are precepts of God impossible for the just to observe. God does not ask the impossible, but by His command, instructs you to do what you are able, to pray for what you are not able that He may help you.'"

In fact, when you stood before God's altar and received the sacrament of matrimony, you received not only graces at that time, but you were guaranteed that you would have all the graces you would need to live successfully in this state for your entire lifetime. Pope Pius XI said that marriage is "a sacrament whose efficacy lasts forever." If married couples seek God's grace by prayer, frequent reception of the sacraments and frequent reflection upon the rights and duties of their state in life, they will gain strength to make a success of their union not only on a material level but also to model their union along the lines of the love Christ had for the Church and the Church had for Christ.

In the little Mystical Body of Christ which is the Christian home, the husband loves his wife as Our Lord loved: With kindness, generosity, and a spirit of self-sacrifice even to the point where He gave His life for it. And a wife loves her husband as the Church loves Our Lord: By complete and utter devotion, by making sacrifices to prove herself worthy of his love, by doing the work of educating his children.

When Our Lord made marriage a sacrament, He made the family a channel through which His graces could flow to men. These graces can make you more successful husbands and wives, fathers and mothers, than you have ever thought possible. But you must place your trust in God, make use of the sacraments and prayer, and seek to develop a higher level of spiritual life for yourself and your family.

Trust in Providence does not mean that one can sit back and wait for God to do all. The Creator knows what our lives will involve, and He has given us the energies and intelligence to provide for ourselves. Because of our limitations, however, we cannot do everything. We are literally God's partners in this work of living Christian lives—and this very idea implies that we must ask Him for help when our own resources are unequal to the tasks we face. A partner does not do everything; neither does he do nothing.

As Christians, nevertheless, we recognize that God knows more than we do. God sees ahead for a lifetime and knows that what we want may not be good for us, while what we do not want may be exactly what we need. Most of us, reviewing our lives, can recall incidents that seemed like tragedies or successes at the time but turned out later to be exactly the opposite. God alone knows that this event today, which seems as unappealing, may prove to be our salvation; or that what we yearn for so ardently could lead to our ruination. With our limited sense of prophecy, we must trust in God's Providence.

Yet He wants us to use our intelligence, too—to exercise the virtue of prudence. We are expected to direct our actions in an intelligent way, bearing in mind the great truth that "the heart has reasons that the mind knows not."

The prudent man need not wear sackcloth and ashes. Neither should he be like the pagans who are unwilling to endure hardship or to make difficult choices. The virtue of prudence follows a middle road.

GRACE CAN WORK MIRACLES

One never ceases to be surprised at the miracles wrought by the infusion of grace in marriage. By virtue of God's grace, young men and women who seem to be poorly equipped for marriage manage to become not only good husbands and wives, but exemplary fathers and mothers as well. Love, on both supernatural and natural levels, transforms them from essentially selfish persons completely concerned about their own pleasure, into persons truly dedicated to each other and to the children they bring into the world. Before they were often unwilling to make even the slightest sacrifice for others. Now they are exemplars of self-sacrifice, performing not only ordinary acts of unselfishness which are necessary for any marriage to survive, but also acts of heroism which enable them to carry burdens which are placed upon few.

For example, there was the youth who at eighteen was interested in nothing but automobiles and "good times." Now thirty-three, he is the father of three children and the husband of a wife with a disease which requires her to spend much time in a sanitarium. Had it not been for the graces of his marriage, this man might have deserted his wife and children, and it would have been in keeping with his character of fifteen years ago. But, working in its own mysterious way, grace has transformed him into a self-sacrificing and devoted husband and a dutiful father who strives to set a good spiritual example to his children.

The mysterious workings of grace can be seen in the family with five children whose father suffered an almost unbelievable series of economic reverses. This family is one of the poorest in the community, yet the parents and children are always smiling: There is sometimes an absence of meat upon the table but never of love upon the hearth. This poorest of families is also one of the happiest—thanks to the grace of God which enables both husband and the wife to realize that things of the spirit are more precious than any that money can buy.

One can also see ample evidence of the workings of grace in the history of the old man and his wife who recently knelt before Francis Cardinal Spellman, Archbishop of New York, to receive his Golden Anniversary Award in the presence of their eight children and most of their thirty grandchildren on the fiftieth anniversary of their marriage. The old man was asked what he remembered most about the fifty years.

His answer was prompt. "The hard work. We never had enough money. But I wouldn't change a bit of it. What man can go to his grave richer than one who leaves behind a priest, a doctor, and other wonderful children? They will be my epitaph."

The grace of God as it works with those who look to Him for help, was also illustrated beautifully at a Cana Conference. During a question-and-answer period, the priest conducting the conference noticed a man sitting in the front of the hall with his wife, who was obviously pregnant. During an informal discussion, the priest asked the man how many children they already had. The husband replied that when the new baby arrived within a month or so, they would have six.

The man and woman were neatly dressed, but obviously their clothing was not of the latest mode. It was also apparent from their demeanor that they were not wealthy or even members of the middle class of society. The priest therefore asked whether they thought they could afford another child.

The husband hesitated momentarily, then replied that they couldn't. "But," he said, "we couldn't afford our fifth, our fourth, our third, or our second. And the child we could least afford was our first."

This couple were motivated by trust of God. But they knew that they too had to do their share of work in the partnership. They recognized that they could not simply sit back and expect fruits to drop from heaven. So their decision to have this child was also motivated by the use of reason and by the virtue of prudence which told them that while it would require some heroism on their part to care for the child and some sacrifice by their other children as well, they would by no means be unable to shoulder the new responsibility.

Millions of couples are leading similar lives of dedication to the principles of their faith. It would be false indeed to think that but a few heroes are scattered among many so-called Christians. In fact, as one sees the churches with many persons at the altar rail, one can realize that there is indeed a tremendous and vital force for Christianity today.

WHAT CHRISTIAN COUPLES
HAVE IN COMMON

Couples who observe the spirit as well as the letter of the natural law and the teachings of the Church generally have five things in common:

1. They clearly understand why they are living as they are. They have the proper motivation. They know that God expects chastity of them regardless of their circumstances, and that they must regulate their own sexual desires in accordance with the right reason which God has given them. They realize full well that when they undertook the vocation of marriage they made a solemn promise to do the work of parenthood. Moreover, they realize why the practice of periodic abstinence is the only legitimate way by which the size of their families can be limited.

They are not troubled by doubts about the course to pursue for very long, because they can always relate their decisions to one question: "What does God want us to do?" They know that any course of action contrary to the law of God would be impossible to follow—that temporary pleasure that might result from such a course would turn to ashes in their mouths. They know that the only lasting satisfaction in life comes from the knowledge that they have done their duty, and that true joy is not achieved by easy comforts, but from the peace of soul and mind which comes from doing one's job as well as one is able.

Their response is like that of the husband and wife who had seven children, and who seemed to be having a constant struggle to provide for them. One time, a rich acquaintance stopped the wife on the street to chat. During the conversation, she asked whether the woman regretted having so many children, so much work, and so few comforts.

The mother answered simply: "Bringing up seven children is not the easiest job in the world. But I can't think of a more satisfying one."

2. They believe in the goodness of God, which means that they believe that He will not give them a job beyond their strength. They believe the old Irish proverb, "When God closes the door, He always opens a window." They believe that faith indeed has the power to move mountains, and they believe the words of Jesus, "If thou canst believe, all things are possible to him who believes." (Mark, 9:22.)

3. They make full use of all the aids which God makes available. Through prayer and meditation and frequent reception of the sacraments, God's graces pour down upon them and enable them to achieve wonders with their lives —to reach levels of achievement which astonish all who know them, as well as themselves.

They believe that when they administered the sacrament of matrimony to each other, they gave each other keys to the storehouse of grace—a storehouse upon which they can draw for help in performing the work of their vocation. They regard the Holy Eucharist as food for their souls, as important to them as is food for their bodies. They partake frequently of the Sacrament of Penance and examine their consciences often, for in this way they remind themselves of their basic purposes in life.

4. They strengthen themselves by taking part in Christian community life. While they are in the world and cannot shut themselves off from its influences, they recognize that its standards are not those by which Christians can lead successful family lives.

So they build their lives around the Christian community in which they live. They make themselves active in Church affairs, interest themselves in the Christian Family Movement, make friends of those with ideals and interests similar to their own. In effect, they create a core of Christian living that is able to resist the pressures and influences of the outside world. Just as the early Christians drew inspiration and strength from each other and so were able to resist the Roman persecutions, so too do modern Christians by associating with one another ward off the siren calls of secularism which are heard on all sides.

They realize that the Christian life often will be difficult, and that Our Lord never promised a life of ease to those He called to follow Him. He made no exception when He said: "If anyone wishes to come after Me, let him deny himself, and take up his cross daily, and follow Me. For he who would save his life will lose it; but he who loses his life for My sake will save it. For what does it profit a man, if he gains the whole world, but ruin or lose himself? For whoever is ashamed of Me and My words, of him will the Son of Man be ashamed when He comes in His glory and that of the Father and of the holy angels." (Luke, 9:23–26.)

5. Above all, today's Christian is sustained by the knowledge that when all is said and done, he is doing a work

which pleases God, and that he will go to God at the end of his days to receive his reward for using his life as God wished him to do. He understands why he was put on earth. He realizes no less than the Christian in the catacombs of early Rome, that the things of this life will pass away, and that the real proof of successful life will come when he can respond to the call of Our Lord on the Day of Judgment: "Come, ye blessed of my Father."

Index